FOOTPRINTS AROUND THE GLOBE

a memoir

BY

LOU ANN SKINNER

Interior photographs © Lou Ann Skinner

Cover and Book design: Vladimir Verano Third Place Press

Author Contact:
laskinner@comcast.net

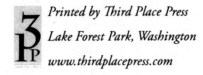

Printed by Third Place Press
Lake Forest Park, Washington
www.thirdplacepress.com

My memoir is dedicated to those friends and colleagues who shared footprints with me as we traveled the globe in our quest for more understanding of the world we live in.

To Jamie —
Hope you
enjoy my "memories"
If I publish the next book —
there'll be more stories
of life in Korea.
Enjoy
Jan Ann (Skinner)

TABLE OF CONTENTS

DISCLAIMER

Readers of this memoir should expect the truth—or as close to the truth as I remember it. It is nonfiction and is written from my memory of travels and life experiences. However, it's known that memories are sometimes flawed and imperfect; mine included. It's impossible to recall all conversations word for word; easy to forget minor details, exact locations, climate and road conditions, and the like.

Even so, this is not a work of fiction. Places, events, characters, and time elements are authentic. Only names have been changed, except for celebrities and those that shared these adventures who are now deceased. However, in the acknowledgements I have mentioned names of friends, whether long departed or still with us, who have shared travel experiences with me. Those friends and fellow educators enriched my travels, my learnings, my life, and thus, my story.

I hope you enjoy the read!

INTRODUCTION

Some 55 years ago, my childhood friend, Sally, planted a seed in my mind when she suggested that I write about my travel adventures and experiences while living outside the United States. That seed was planted in 1960 and I had just returned from living five years in Addis Ababa, Ethiopia. Upon returning to Oklahoma I had settled in Tulsa, which was within an hour of where Sally lived with her family. I was a frequent guest in her home.

During my visits I occasionally shared my adventures with her young family. Her three small children became my favorite audience. It was a delight telling them about my escapades and getting their reactions. Often, the children would crawl up in bed with me and snuggle in as I wove tales for them about my African adventures. Of course I over-dramatized, hoping not only to entertain them but also to scare them (just a little). Lions, jungles, hyenas, picturesque tribesmen, palaces and emperors, my pet monkeys--all of my stories and characters brought squeals, moans and giggles. Out of the corner of my eye, I might see little heads peeking from under pillows or small lumps crawling under the blankets to hide.

As I continued to travel, I gave Sally's suggestion considerable thought. Still, time passed, inertia set in and no writing was accomplished--until last year. A number of factors arose that urged me to get busy and start telling my stories with the hope that family and friends would find them fascinating and entertaining. I remain grateful to this day to Sally for her continuing encouragement through the years to tell those stories. It has been a time-consuming challenge, but a highly worthwhile undertaking. For me, it's been a marvelous trip down Memory Lane, which I've greatly enjoyed. Hopefully, you will too.

The day came when I finally put pen to paper (and yes--computer) and started the challenge of "writing my memoirs." My initial problem was to determine which stories should be told. Through the many years as an educator overseas, and in retirement, I have traveled to roughly 150 countries which include all continents except Antarctica. Each and every excursion has been a marvelous adventure to a world of unknowns. At the time of my visits, some of those countries did not even have organized tours. It was apparent that I couldn't possibly write about all of those unique trips. As a result, I labored over which journeys should be included. After considerable thought I elected to write only about countries not often visited or those that I was fortunate to visit before hordes of tourists descended on them, which invariably changed their way of life.

A few examples that you'll find in the book are compelling stories (I hope) of those five years I spent in teaching and traveling in Ethiopia and other African countries in the 1950s. I never left the African continent in those years. The first few chapters are professional pursuits with which I was fortunate to be involved. Subsequent chapters are related more to travels and the pre-tourism time of my visits. Some examples of those chapters are: going into Yemen in the 50s, to Korea in the 60s, to Sikkim and Nepal in the 70s, or to the Roof of the World and to Papua New Guinea in the 80s. In the 80s and 90s you'll also find, Torajaland, Tibet, and Nepal--to mention but a few. I have not included countries that are normally on a tourist's list of "places to see." Travels in Europe, China, Russia, South and Central America, Europe, the Middle East, and so on, are not addressed. Moreover, I did not include one of my all-time favorite adventures, which was a six-week driving safari in East Africa in the 50s. That trip included an attempt to climb Mt. Kilimanjaro. (I didn't make it to the summit.)

Why, you might ask, didn't you write about that six-week safari? I respond that it is simply because, for one book, I'd had too many other extraordinary and unparalleled experiences. Furthermore, in the ensuing years a great number of people have made and written about their own memorable trips to Africa. Instead, I elected to tell the story of driving overland through the isolated Northern Frontier of Kenya to Ethiopia in a caravan. (A caravan was required because of the dangers in that region and lack of any support services for unexpected difficulties.) This adventure required getting permission from the British District Office in Nairobi. At that time we were told that it would entail using a compass for segments of the trip due to a lack of roads and maps. Such a trip was rarely attempted in the 50s. It made sense to me to tell of that adventure rather than African journeys others had also taken. There were more obstacles in that particular trip than most travelers encounter when visiting Africa these days.

I didn't always have a gypsy foot or wanderlust. Rather, I spent my formative years in the small rural town of Perry, Oklahoma. I had always assumed that after college I would return to live in that small town, or elsewhere in the state. Perry was a wonderful community for my formative years. Our family of five (parents Ralph and Vivian; brothers John and Gay) were all exceptionally involved with school and various community activities. Our home was a gathering place for all ages. Still, after my graduation from high school our family scattered to other places. Each of us often returned to Perry for visits. We all agreed that we could not have grown up in a better hometown.

Childhood was a wholesome one of playing hide-and-seek or "kick the can", catching fireflies, attending church and Sunday school, Boy Scouts, Blue Birds and Campfire Girls, homemade ice cream, sports, piano, and an abundance of other wonderful pursuits. During my high school years I came to realize that music, specifically piano, would be of central importance in my life. Despite the fact that I was involved in a multitude of high school activities the focus was always on music. Always. I participated in Concert Band, Marching Band and Chorus. I competed in Regional and State piano competitions and gave frequent recitals. Working diligently at my craft, I hoped to become a fine pianist and musician.

After graduating from Perry High School, as did my brothers, I left Perry for my freshman year at Oklahoma College for Women with a scholarship in piano. The following year I transferred to the University of Oklahoma where, in due course, I graduated with a Bachelor of Music in Piano, Class of 1955. For two years prior to my graduation, my parents had been living in Ethiopia. They had written with exuberance about their love of living overseas and suggested that I join them after graduation to start my professional career in Ethiopia. I had been offered a three-year contract to teach in Addis Ababa. I was elated at the thought of joining them and living in Africa, but there was a huge complication. I had been dating a fine young man, a musician, and we were beginning to think of marriage. I faced a terrible dilemma. The choice was difficult and painful to make. Our mutual decision was for me to join my parents, take the job offer and he would join me in Ethiopia after one year. Our plan materialized and he did join me, but we never married. We remained friends for years and were in close contact until his untimely death a few years ago.

I signed a contract with the Ethiopian Ministry of Education as the Directress of the School of Music. It was the first and only music school in the country. Let me hasten to add that this facility was a two-room shack, with one piano--and no plumbing. Furthermore, when it rained outside, it rained nearly as much inside! It was said that in all of Ethiopia there were only 10 pianos (other than those in the Palaces and Embassies) and the School of Music was fortunate to have one of those 10 pianos.

The educational objective of the School of Music was to teach young students to play the piano or violin. This was truly a ridiculous concept when one considered that some of the students had no shoes, no shirts and certainly no piano or violin. They could not have afforded instruments of any kind. Needless to say this impractical goal of teaching piano or violin was soon modified to include choral music. The voice is affordable and easy to carry with you! It was a more realistic objective. In 1996 when I returned to Ethiopia, it was heartening to see that a new music school had replaced the old, original one. Happily, it had plumbing and the roof didn't leak! I had a small part in drawing the plans for that new school, and was delighted to see that it had come to fruition. Rewarding!

I taught in Africa for five years without leaving the continent except for Yemen. After that, I returned to Oklahoma and started my stateside teaching career in Tulsa, Oklahoma, at the Billy Mitchell Elementary School. I enjoyed it, but "gypsy fever" was still in my blood and I eventually applied for a teaching position with the Department of Defense Dependent Schools. I was accepted and my first assignment was in Goose Bay, Labrador, followed by Seoul, Korea, where I remained until my retirement. As a music teacher and guidance counselor, I was rewarded with the rare opportunity of seeing the world and experiencing unimaginable adventures. I thrived on it!

It is my fervent hope that you'll enjoy reading about these escapades as much as I have had in recalling and writing about them. I regret that I could only describe highlights of each trip because of the necessity to limit the numerous stories that I could relate. To go into any more detail or tell additional stories would be too exhaustive for the reader, as it would be for me, the writer. Perhaps in the future I'll put pen to paper again for a second go-around…

PART I

MAGICAL YEARS
IN AFRICA-YEMEN

Chapter 1

THE KING AND I

*T*he King and I... Really? No, not really. However, my adventure
could easily be titled, "The Emperor and I"! Let me start at the
beginning.

I lived in Ethiopia for five amazing years. Those years were filled
with extraordinary adventures and opportunities to meet unique
and inspiring people. This is an account of one of my first incredible
experiences.

A few years after I arrived in Addis Ababa in the mid-50s, His
Imperial Majesty, Haile Selassie's favorite son, the Duke of Harare
was killed in an automobile accident. As a result of this tragic event
the American community in Addis Ababa, which was composed
of approximately 300 employees of various U.S. agencies, resolved
to give a memorial concert in memory of His Majesty's son. I had
arrived in Addis a few months earlier (recently graduated from the
University of Oklahoma with a degree in Piano) and was asked to
perform for this auspicious occasion. Of course, I was elated at being
asked and jumped at the opportunity. There were other Americans
who also performed, so it was an honor to be requested to perform
the final selection on the program. (In addition to other selections,
the final piece I performed was Gershwin's Rhapsody in Blue.) To
be expected, His Majesty was present—which made for me—a performance of a lifetime!

A week or so after the performance, the significance of the Memorial Concert became apparent. I received a call from the Palace requesting that I come to the school building on the Palace grounds to discuss giving music lessons to His Majesty's grandchildren. I was overwhelmed! After meeting with the British couple who were vested with the responsibility of the grandchildren's education and then going through significant bureaucracies to obtain necessary documentation for entrance to the Palace grounds—I was ready to go! An amazing adventure was about to begin.

On that first day, I drove my beige Volkswagen Beetle to the front gates of the Palace and was greeted by two guardsmen who approached my car with rifles in hand—pointed directly at me! After trying to communicate with my limited Amharic (national language of the country) and handing them the papers that were necessary for admittance, the gigantic metal gates of the Palace finally swung open. I drove through the gates and up a paved road for about 35 yards until I came to a small building, adjacent to the Palace. This building was the school where the children had their lessons. (The nearby Palace was a large, imposing structure but not nearly as ostentatious as one might expect.) I parked the car, got out and started walking toward the school. I had not gone far when I abruptly stopped in my tracks! Why? To my left, perhaps 30 yards away was a magnificent LION! Imagine—just imagine! It was a well-known fact that His Majesty, also referred to as the "Lion of Judah," kept two lions on the Palace grounds that were cared for by two attendants. I could see a lion—but, where, oh where were the attendants? Not to be seen!

For a few seconds I hesitated not knowing what to do. After what seemed an eternity, I started backing slowly toward my car, keeping a keen eye on the lion. It had continued watching me but mercifully, had not moved. Suddenly, I heard a voice nearby and saw an Ethiopian coming toward me with a big grin on his face.

He said something to me in his native Amharic language which I translated to mean "It's OK, it's OK! Don't be afraid." Under the circumstances, it was an absurd and even comical statement!

The next happening was even more unbelievable! In a series of gestures and words and with an encouraging and friendly manner, he led me over to Mr. Lion. It was obvious that he was offering me the opportunity to touch—to pet—Mr. Lion. I was speechless! Of course, not being a timid soul, I slowly reached out, extending my arm as far as it could possibly be extended—and I touched Mr. Lion. Astonishing! Unimaginable! Fortunately, Mr. Lion remained quiet, hardly moving at all except to shake his massive mane a couple of times.

After spending a moment or so with him, it was time to go to the school house. I was a little disappointed having seen Mr. Lion close-up. He was not a picture-perfect specimen like we see in movies and photographs, but rather a dirty, mangy, unhealthy-looking lion. I had seen this lion on several occasions as His Majesty often rode in an open jeep with one or both lions at his side. From a distance they always looked picture-perfect. Nevertheless, my meeting with dirty, mangy Mr. Lion was a never-to-be forgotten experience that I will always cherish!

Having become acquainted with Mr. Lion that day, I continued on to the school for the first music lessons with the children. I didn't ever see Mr. Lion again while on the Palace grounds. The music lessons continued for several years, as did the lessons I gave at the Crown Prince's Palace.

I became curious about what had happened to His Majesty's grandchildren after their family had been exiled. With a little research, the internet came up with some answers. The findings were unexpected and shocking. After the Emperor's death, his son the Crown Prince was heir apparent to the throne. Following the Crown

Prince's demise, his son, Zera Yacob Amha Selassie, became Head of the Imperial House of Ethiopia and is currently recognized as such by the Crown Counsel of Ethiopia. Yacob is one of the children I had taught. After receiving his education at Eton and Oxford, Yacob lived briefly in both England and the U.S. At this time he resides in Addis Ababa and has for many years. It's been fun to think that, at one time, I taught the present Crowned Head of Ethiopia. Even so, I remember him as an adorable, handsome and chubby youngster who seldom practiced his music lessons—and could hardly find "Middle C" on the piano!

It should be noted that the Crown Princess requested a monthly report on the progress of her children in piano. (Actually, none of the children ever practiced or found "Middle C" with ease.) Regardless, I appeared in her living quarters to discuss their piano lessons and—as diplomatically as possible—gave honest, but unhappily negative reports. I remain firmly convinced that the "reports" were a device of the Crown Prince, to make sure that his wife had the opportunity to practice her English.

A few years ago a friend saw a picture of a lion on the front steps of the Imperial Palace. The picture was said to have been taken in the fifties and reflected an old, scruffy and unhealthy looking animal. I like to believe that it was my old friend, Mr. Lion.

Chapter 2

THE STATE DINNER:
THE VP IS COMING!

I had heard rumors that Vice President Richard Nixon was coming for an official meeting with His Majesty. It would be the first time that an official that high in the United States government had ever visited Ethiopia! The American community was certainly thrilled over the prospects of this visit, as were most educated Ethiopians. At that time in Ethiopia, the illiteracy rate was approximately 97%. It could be presumed that, living in the outer provinces, few Ethiopians had ever seen a publication of any kind, or even knew of the existence of a country known as the United States.

A phone call came from the office of the Ambassador's wife, Mrs. Simpson, requesting that I come to her office to discuss the music that would be performed at the State Dinner during Mr. Nixon's visit. At that consultation it was decided that soft background music should be played while dinner was served. A baby grand would be situated near the dining table for that purpose. She also requested additional music selections to be performed when the guests retired to the drawing room for coffee and dessert. I left that meeting with mixed emotions: apprehension, excitement, humility, and enthusiasm—quite a range of feelings and thoughts evolved.

In the weeks that followed my head was in a whirl with issues that needed to be resolved before this memorable event. What piano selections would be appropriate? What special music would be suitable while coffee and dessert was being served? What was the proper dress for this auspicious occasion? Many concerns had to be considered. I was acutely aware that I had been given an opportunity of a lifetime. Still, as wonderful as it was, it carried the weight of responsibility.

Several weeks later, after making piano selections and preparing a vocal trio for the after-dinner performance, we were ready to go! I was very fortunate to know two friends in the American community who had formal vocal training and had fantastic voices. Thus, it was decided that the three of us would perform several vocal trio selections. David, a close friend of mine who was an excellent pianist accompanied us. We had many conversations and great fun in preparing for this very special event. A significant amount of time was spent trying to decide what attire we'd wear. Long or short gowns? Shoes? Hair-styles? Make-up? All that "girly stuff" was nearly as important to us as the presentation of the music.

The night of this extraordinary occasion finally arrived. It was March 1957 and a car from the Embassy arrived to take us to the Embassy grounds. We were *elated*! We arrived at the Ambassador's residence to see that a red carpet had literally been rolled out, covering the stairs and on up to the entrance to the great reception hall. On each side of the red carpet were two Marines resplendent in their "dress blues" and standing at attention. They looked very regal.

We were escorted up the stairs and into the residence where our wraps were taken. We were guided to an area near the formal dining room and were served dinner while the guests were arriving. There were twenty in attendance: The Emperor, the Empress, the Crown Prince, the Crown Princess, Princess Mary and her husband, the United States Operation Mission Director and his wife, and a few others that I can't name—and of course, Ambassador Simpson and his wife.

A few moments before the guests were escorted to the dining room, I was requested to take my place at the piano and start the music. The room was dimly lit so I only had time to glance at the dining table. It was elegantly set with china, crystal, silver and it glowed in the candle light. (Unfortunately, I do not remember any selections I played during that dinner, but I do remember having given a lot of thought to making those selections.)

During the dinner I was close enough to hear the guests conversing, but was not near enough to determine if any important topics were being discussed. Probably not. After dinner the guests were escorted to the stately drawing room and comfortably seated on couches and chairs. I noticed that there was an American flag and on the walls were photographs of previous Ambassadors. After a brief interlude, we were "on stage." We performed three selections—all very light. I remember only one selection that was performed and it was "Without a Song" (1929, Music: Vincent Youmans; Lyrics: Billy Rose and Edward Eliscu). I do remember that our trio had had long discussions on what was to be performed. I think our musical efforts were appreciated because the applause was significant.

What transpired next was completely unexpected. The Vice President came over to thank us personally! Fantastic! He stood and chatted with us for perhaps five minutes. Unbelievable! Mrs. Nixon remained on the couch talking with the Ambassador's wife, so we did not have the opportunity to talk to her. But, I do remember she looked lovely. She was dressed in a dark pink gown and with her gray-blond hair she was striking. It was apparent that she was friendly, engaged and enjoying those around her.

After talking with the Vice President, the time had come to leave. A servant escorted us to get our wraps and we departed from the building. The Marines were still standing at full attention, the red carpet was still in place, and our chariot was waiting at the foot of the stairs. Our Cinderella experience was over!

I received letters from the Vice President and the Ambassador thanking me for my assistance in making the official State Dinner such a success. I still have those letters—framed and hanging on the wall of my home in Bothell.

Emperor Haile Selassie's grandchildren.
Yacob is on the far left. He is recognized as the head of the
Inperial Household and resides in Addis Ababa, Ethiopia.

OFFICE OF THE VICE PRESIDENT

WASHINGTON

March 15, 1957

Dear Miss Skinner:

     This is just a note to tell you how much Mrs. Nixon and I, as well as the other members of our party, enjoyed the musical program of your group after dinner at the Ambassador's residence. The pleasant harmony put just the right touch to the end of a very nice evening.

     Please convey our thanks to the other members of the group and accept the best wishes of Mrs. Nixon and myself for the future.

            Sincerely,

            Richard Nixon

Miss Lou Ann Skinner
c/o American Embassy
Addis Ababa, Ethiopia

*An acknowledgement from Vice-President
Nixon after the State dinner.*

His Imperial Highness the Crown Prince
Merid Azmatch Asfa Wossen

President of the Ethiopian Red Cross Society

kindly requests the attendance of

Miss Lor Ann Skinner

to the Hundredth Anniversary of World Red Cross

at the Haile Selassie 1st Theatre, on Saturday the 27th of June, 1959

at 8.00 p. m.

Black tie

Please show this invitation card at the door

Entrance Free

(Concert and Champagne - Cocktail)

*One of the several invitations received from
the wife of the Crown Prince.*

American Embassy,
Addis Ababa, Ethiopia,
November 26, 1956.

Dear Miss Skinner:

Your contribution again this year to the annual American
Thanksgiving Day service was very much appreciated. I want you
to know that not only I personally but all of us Americans here
are grateful for your willingness to participate in events of
this kind in our American community. You helped very materi-
ally to make this annual observance of the American Thanksgiving Day an outstanding one for us even though we are far away
from home.

Sincerely yours,

Joseph Simonson
United States Ambassador

Miss Lou Ann Skinner,
    USOM, American Embassy,
        Addis Ababa, Ethiopia.

A thank you from the U. S. Ambassador for a music presentation.

Chapter 3

CHRISTMAS EVE AT THE PALACE

His Imperial Majesty, Haile Selassie, had a great respect and fondness for Americans. This was demonstrated in his annual Christmas Eve party to which he invited all Americans in the community to the Palace to share this special season.

We all assembled at the American Embassy and traveled in caravan to the Palace. I was responsible for the special vocal ensemble pieces that would be performed (before actually entering the Palace). Therefore, my car was fourth in line of the caravan—after the Ambassador and his *entourage*. It was necessary that I arrive at the Palace a little before the crowd arrived in order to set up a small pump organ. It would be used to accompany the special vocal selections and for group caroling. We transferred the organ from the car to a place near the balcony, while the crowd gathered around us. You could actually feel the anticipation of the participants!

All of us were eagerly looking forward to the Emperor's appearance on the balcony and the festivities that would follow. Without a great deal of fanfare, the balcony doors opened and the Emperor appeared in his customary full military regalia. With him were a few members of the Royal Family and several aides. We greeted them enthusiastically. Most Americans that resided in Ethiopia had great respect for His Imperial Majesty (HIM) and the extraordinary accomplishments he had achieved for his country. Their excitement also reflected gratitude for having been invited to the Palace on this holiday night. His Majesty simply smiled—but a few younger family members waved to acknowledge our presence.

It was now time for our "gift" of music to him. The sextet (a group of six musicians) had prepared a couple of well-known Christmas carols. They sang beautifully and were well-received by His Majesty and his family. Finally, it was time for the last music selection—the Christmas carol that all the Americans were nervous about singing. In past years, and again this year, His Majesty requested that his favorite Christmas carol, Silent Night, be sung in Amharic, his native language. Of course, there had been no rehearsal for this presentation, although a paper with Amharic words had been given to each person present. Unfortunately, we stumbled and mumbled through the music but finally made it through the first two verses. I doubt that His Majesty recognized a single world of it! After our dismal performance of Silent Night in Amharic, we cheerfully finished with the singing of the first verse of Silent Night in English. His Majesty, always very gracious, clapped his hands vigorously—as did those who were on the balcony with him.

After the singing of Silent Night, he and his *entourage* left the balcony. Then the great fun of this memorable night began! The doors to the entrance of the Palace were opened and we were ushered in, passing through a reception hall to the *throne room*. The interior of the Palace that we were able to see was rather austere, unlike the ostentatious palaces in Europe. It was a long rectangle-shaped room, not at all ornate or impressive and with a smattering of pictures and portraits on the walls. There was an enormous red carpet about 10 yards wide and 35 yards long, which ran from the entrance of the room to the other end and up a few steps to the throne itself. The throne was simple: an enormous wooden chair with what appeared to be heavy drapery, or similar fabric, thrown over the back of it.

The arms of the chair were exposed and at the end of each arm a lion's head had been carved.

As we were gathering in the throne room, His Majesty and those with him appeared and he was escorted up to his throne. It was an exhilarating time for us! Waiters dressed in *shamus* (the national dress of Ethiopia) circulated around the room with trays of champagne and finger foods—including caviar! I do not remember if other drinks were served, but it wasn't a problem as we were all thrilled to be in the Palace. It was to be expected that a lot of imbibing was taking place. It was a very festive and happy occasion! After all, how often is one invited to a palace on Christmas Eve—and to share it with the Crowned Head of the country? It was absolutely astonishing!

After a brief time, His Majesty came down the few stairs and stopped to talk with guests. I was one of the fortunate ones, in that I was presented to the Emperor as his grandchildren's music teacher. What a thrill! Even though I had been going to the school house on the Palace grounds to give music lessons, I had never had the honor of being presented to him. After circulating and exchanging pleasantries with his guests, the Emperor returned to the throne and was seated again.

Perhaps a half-hour later, the storybook evening ended and it was time to depart. The party was over! But wait! That's exactly when the comic aspects of the evening began. Ethiopian tradition is that no one ever turns his or her back on the Emperor. This night was no exception. Consequently, it was necessary first to curtsy or bow, and then to start the long, long, long backing-up ritual to the other end of the room in order to depart the "Presence" on the throne. There were many hilarious aspects of this farce. For one thing, most Americans had little or no experience in bowing or curtseying. For another, backing out of a room on a red carpet for 35 yards in the presence of Royalty when there had been substantial imbibing involved was not for the faint of heart! Needless to say, it was entertaining! You might even say it was a hoot! There were many giggles, snickers, and a profusion of good-natured laughs as we watched our fellow Americans going through this ancient ceremony of leaving the throne room while tipsy. Fun!

Our Christmas Eve with the Emperor at the Imperial Palace had ended. We staggered and stumbled out to our cars; each lost in our own thoughts of the fairy-tale event that we had just experienced!

Chapter 4

LALIBELA: MONOLITHIC CHURCHES OF ETHIOPIA

The year was 1957, when I made what remains one of the most unbelievable adventures of my lifetime. I made a trip to the Monolithic Churches of Lalibela. This is an account of that trip.

Our group of six decided to make a trip into the jungle that no other Americans had ever attempted. (To our knowledge, only one German woman had previously made the trip.) The six of us were all under the age of forty, except one Canadian woman in her early forties. Our ensemble included four Americans and two Canadians. We were three guys and three gals. In addition to us, the Imperial Palace sent a few guards with rifles for security reasons. This was absurd in that the rifles the guides carried were of ancient vintage and could not be trusted to protect us from any living creature. There was only one other gun taken and it was a pistol that I was selected to carry. I've never understood why I had the "honor" of carrying the weapon. I had only fired a gun once or twice in my lifetime; I knew I could not be counted on to protect us from any harm whatsoever.

We had numerous planning sessions. These sessions were of great importance. We fully realized that once we left our cars in civilization and started into the jungle, we would have to trust our own resources for survival. We had to take *all* essential provisions with us: food, limited jugs full of water, tents, medicines (to include iodine pills for water purification) and other basic necessities. For 10-12 hours a day, we would be traveling by donkey or mule into the jungle, also known as "the bush." Adequate preparations were fundamental to success of the trip.

It was another beautiful day in Ethiopia when we assembled for our much anticipated adventure. Ethiopia has an average temperature of 75 degrees Fahrenheit year-round; important to us since we didn't have to worry about the rains or inclement weather. In addition to our adventuresome group and the Palace guards (with their trusty guns) a young Ethiopian by name of Getachew also came along to help us, as needed. He was later to become the VIP of our trip, and one might add—to a lesser degree—our survival. Hargus, my Dad's driver, also accompanied us and was used as our much-needed interpreter.

We left Addis Ababa, the capital city, at a very early hour and drove in Land-Rovers for six or seven hours over indescribably unpaved roads to Wolde, a small Ethiopian village. It was in this village that we were to meet our guides and gather the donkeys and mules that would carry us and our gear up to the churches. The guides would handle the animals and lead us to Lalibela. They were also needed to help us get on and off the donkeys and mules; an activity which we were soon to discover was not easy. Few of us had ever spent any time on horses, donkeys or mules, and none of us could mount them unassisted. We unloaded our needed provisions. Guides then loaded our gear on the "beasts of burden," and off we went up through the mountains toward our destination.

Ethiopia is known as the "Switzerland of Africa." Its highest mountain peak reaches 15,000 feet. We were quick to realize that our journey would be considerably more strenuous and hazardous than we had anticipated. We rode for about six hours that first day and when we finally made camp that night we were totally exhausted! Not only were we stiff and sore, but also we discovered it was not easy to walk after spending hours and hours in the saddle! Unfortunately for us, we knew our arduous day was not yet over; we still had to put up our tents, prepare something to eat, wash up, and attend to other necessities. It was a tough, tough day, but in retrospect it was one of the easier days of our journey.

The next three days we rode on treacherous mountain trails, usually riding 10-12 hours a day. That evening when we finally arrived at our destination of Lalibela, we were exhausted but in good spirits. After making camp that night we put our heads together to decide our itinerary for exploration of the churches. After a lengthy discussion, we went to our tents—happy that we would remain in one place. We would not have to set up camp again, nor spend as much time on our four-legged means of transportation.

The following day we awoke to unfortunate news. We were shocked to learn that Pauline (a strong and healthy woman in our group) had difficulty getting out of bed that morning and was in considerable pain. It was evident that we had to address this unexpected problem as soon as possible. What to do? After conferring, we considered assembling a stretcher of some sort to carry her back over the trails we had traveled. But, after more realistic discussions, we knew that would not be possible. The topography was simply too treacherous—much too dangerous to even attempt it. A decision was finally made that we would send Getachew back to the nearest means of communication to alert the American Embassy that we were stranded on a mountain near Lalibela, and that a member in our travel party was ill, in great pain and could not travel any further. We prepared a message telling of our situation and requesting medicines and food that would be needed if we were to remain longer in that area.

Getachew left the next day on what was thought to be the strongest and fastest donkey. Pauline, who was still in considerable distress, was adamant that she would be safe in camp, and that we should follow the agreed itinerary to explore Lalibela. With some trepidation we left her in her tent. Hargus, our interpreter stayed to care for her, as needed. The next few days we explored the historical Monolithic Churches of Lalibela—without our friend.

The churches of Lalibela are medieval underground sculptures dating from the 12th century. It is said they were hewn out of rock by the hand of King Lalibela with an army of helpers. (There are still 11 churches which are interconnected, plus a few independent churches several hours away.) Some appeared to have been dropped from the sky into deep, enormous pits. Others were carved out of rock at ground level. Interiors of the churches had no electricity, few windows, and occasionally water dripped from roof-tops into large jugs. This water was then considered "holy water." We some-times had to crawl around on hands and knees from one church to another. Not pleasant! Walls inside were interspersed with colorful religious art and a few churches had bones scattered on dirt and mud floors. Priests in ornate, colorful robes were quietly praying or reading goatskin bibles. Monks lived in nearby caves. My favorite church was Biet Giorgis—which if viewed from the sky is shaped like a cross. It was at this church that we had the immense honor of meeting the Abuna, High Priest of Lalibela. The Abuna was consid-ered to be the equivalent of the Pope. It was generally understood that this complex of Monolithic Churches was the "Vatican of Ethiopian Orthodox Christianity."

On the third day after Getachew left, he reached a police station that had a radio, which was the nearest method of communication with the "outside world." Contact was made with the Embassy tell-ing them of our dire circumstances. Thus, on the fourth day, we heard sounds in the distant sky. Happily, it was a plane! As the plane descended natives became increasingly agitated, even panicked. It was apparent that some had never seen or heard a plane before. The plane circled and dropped a small container with a message saying that food and other provisions would be dropped and to clear the field. More important, a helicopter would be sent to evacuate Pauline when one could be located, hopefully in four or five days. We were elated to know that help was on the way for Pauline, who was still suffering and needed medical attention. Several days later we again heard sounds from the sky. We were ecstatic when we viewed the speck in the sky. It was the much-anticipated helicopter! Natives stood and watched in awe as this "monster", the helicopter, descended. After it touched the ground, we half-walked, half-carried Pauline gently to the aircraft. The rotary blades continued their rotation as Pauline was helped aboard.

After it lifted off pandemonium broke out! Natives began running, screaming, frantically trying to hide behind trees, under bushes, in crevices; some were even running into our tents to "escape the monster." It was an unforgettable spectacle! After a measure of calmness prevailed, our interpreter talked with the natives and asked them, "Why are you afraid?" Their response was that they were afraid that the "big bug" would swallow them up and take them away!

Ethiopians celebrate Christmas on or around January 7, based on the Julian calendar. On this hallowed and sacred day, we made our last visit to these underground places of worship. We returned to Biet Giorgis—the church shaped like a gigantic cross. As we came nearer to the church, we could see and hear in the distance a multitude of natives that had gathered for their annual gift of alms from His Majesty. We were curious about this throng of people but continued on to the church. Upon arrival, we dismounted our animals and walked down a trench-like trail, in a circular direction, to the base of the church—perhaps three or four stories from ground level. We spent a couple of hours exploring and attempting to communicate with several priests and monks, and a few other Ethiopians who had come to worship. Eventually the time came to leave—much too soon.

We walked back up the circular trail, mounted our mules, and were taken over to the swarm of natives we had seen upon our arrival. (It was estimated that there were a thousand or more assembled.) As we came nearer, an unforgettable sight came into view. There were hordes and hordes of natives, with every known disease, ailment, malady, and disorder known to mankind. There were the blind and those without an arm or leg, or both. There were those who had leprosy in various stages of development. They were of all ages: young, old, middle aged, and babies. All were in dirty, filthy rags and a few without clothes. It was a wretched scene; beyond words to describe—heartbreaking! Twenty or thirty skinny, unhealthy looking donkeys were standing nearby with large, leather saddlebags thrown over their backs. From these bags, money (called *birr*), was being distributed by representatives of the Governor of the Providence at the order of His Imperial Majesty. The natives were not unruly; standing in line until it was time to step forward and receive their alms. There was a continual anguished wailing—which was as heartbreaking as was the sight of those destitute, vulnerable people in their hopeless situation.

It was a tough, tough spectacle that we had encountered. We didn't stay long and as we left, there were tears shed, reflecting incredible sorrow at what we had just witnessed. Few words were spoken on our trip back to camp, each trying to come to terms with the magnitude of the unspeakable poverty we had just seen. It was quiet in camp that night. We sat around the campfire each lost in thought, and after a time, we silently went to our tents.

The following day we packed up our tents and belongings and started the long, strenuous journey back over the mountains to Wolde—to civilization (and our cars). At this time it was important to each of us to get home as quickly as possible. There was a sense of desperation in us, to sleep in our own beds, drink clean water without iodine pills, have a good hot meal, and to relish, enjoy and SPEND *HOURS* in a HOT BATH!

As we drove from Wolde back to Addis Ababa, on that last day of our odyssey, we fully realized that we had experienced a unique adventure that was unlikely—ever—to be equaled in our lifetimes.

A few more unexpected happenings took place on this journey and are worth mentioning.

Most natives in this area had never seen Caucasians. They timidly came up to touch us, even rubbing our skin to see if the "white" would disappear.

Often, since I was the only blonde on the trip, I was cautiously approached by the natives wanting to touch my "golden hair." Fun!

It should be mentioned that most Ethiopians had little access to water, and most likely had never had what we call a "bath" *in their entire lives.* Consequently, when in close proximity one always knew to expect interesting odors permeating the air.

After our return to Addis Ababa, the Ambassador requested a briefing concerning our expedition and requested our recommendations for future adventurers. One suggestion was that any woman over the age of 40 be discouraged from making this trip. Joy, the 40-year-old Canadian, had great difficulty throughout the trip. It was too much of a physical challenge for her—far too demanding! She concurred with our assessment. However, as I reflect back on this trip from the vantage point of being an active world traveler in my early 80s, I am embarrassed at our youthful recommendation.

Pauline, who had been evacuated from Lalibela by helicopter to the hospital in Addis Ababa, was diagnosed as having slipped discs. The "big bug" had come to transport her from an American military unit stationed in Addis. Pauline recovered, but was never again as adventuresome in her travels.

Lalibela is now on many travel lists as one of the "10 Best Places to See" in the world. It ranks up there with the Pyramids at Giza, Angkor Wat, Machu Picchu, Victoria Falls—and other astonishing tourist sites.

Above: Biet Giorgis.
My favorite church in Lalibela. It's shaped like a cross.

Below: An independent church several kilometers from Biet Giorgis.

*Above: Natives standing on ground-level, peering
down to the courtyard of Biet Giorgis.*

Below: An example of artwork in one of the churches of Lalibela.

Lou Ann with her muleteer/guide on the trail to Lalibela.

Chapter 5

THE "THRONE" LESSON AT
HAILE SELASSIE UNIVERSITY

The School of Music where I was employed was across the street from the Haile Selassie University—and was considered to be the most outstanding institute of learning in Ethiopia. Professors at the university were Jesuit priests and students that attended the university were the brightest in the country. The student body was predominately male.

I had some professional contact with the university and one morning I was alerted that there would be a most unusual assembly that day that I might want to attend. Consequently, I went over to the auditorium. I found that it was crowded but was able to find a seat near the back of the room. The stage curtains were not closed and the stage was totally bare except that in the middle of the stage was set a standard-sized, white porcelain, western-type commode. Amazing!

I began to suspect the purpose of this specific assembly and, stifling a giggle. I prepared myself for what was to come. At this time in Ethiopia, water and electricity were rare in the entire country, and even in the capital city. As a result, there were few western-type commodes and often in the mornings and evenings one could observe "squatters." When nature called—it was a necessity!

Soon after I arrived two professors entered the stage and the assembly began. The first professor gave a short talk on the mechanics and operation of the commode. A great part of his lecture related to personal hygiene, sanitation and the necessity of using a commode when available.

After the first professor finished his instructional statements, the other professor (who was fully clothed in the traditional Jesuit back suit and Roman collar) was ask to sit down on the "contraption." The lid was up, so the professor did as was requested. He sat down on the seat of the commode—fully clothed. Of course, the students roared with laughter at such a spectacle! Fortunately, the professor's instructions and demonstration didn't need to go any further. Students had figured out "what to do."

It was a well-known fact that most Ethiopians, when faced for the first time with this "contraption", simply climbed on top of the seat. With their feet on the rim, they did a balancing act: one foot on one side and the other foot on the opposite side. It made for a very precarious act of nature!

When the laughter died down, the professors had a question and answer session. Regrettably, I had to leave. I've always been sorry that I couldn't stay. I can only imagine how bizarre and outlandish some of those questions might have been.

Nevertheless, the assembly was very instructional for some, if not for most students. In ensuing days, fewer and fewer squatters were seen in the fields—an indication that the "throne" lesson had been well learned.

I can assure you that reflecting on this particular assembly always brings a smile to my face. It is one of those rare assemblies that I will not forget!

Chapter 6

A Buffet Dinner Of
Unexpected "Delicacies"

Another noteworthy experience at the Haile Selassie University was a buffet dinner that I attended. It was evening as I made my way to the university—a beautiful time of the day. The fragrant aroma of numerous eucalyptus trees wafted gently through the air; smoke drifted from the *tukels* (Ethiopian homes) as the evening meal was being prepared; sounds echoed in the distance—donkeys and mules and children at play. It was a kaleidoscope of sounds and smells; like an eerie and mysterious movie that you had accidentally stepped into.

I easily found the banquet hall and my friends were already seated at various tables scattered around the large room. After a short time of visiting, the buffet table was opened. It was time to eat. The long buffet table was laden with an abundance of Ethiopian food: *injera* and *wat* (flatbread and chicken stew, staples of the country), *tibs* (lamb stir-fry), raw beef, a few vegetables, *dabocolo* (traditional bean bread), and other delicacies. It was a feast fit for a "king"—or an Emperor! We took our places in line, filling our plates with whatever appealed to us.

As I approached the end of the table, an item came into view that I didn't quite understand. I took another look and yes, my eyes had not deceived me.

It was indeed a small animal, perhaps two or three feet tall propped on its own legs at the end of the table. I thought, "Whatever on earth is that?" and stepped closer. I could hardly believe my eyes for, as I approached, I realized that it was exactly what I thought it was: a tiny, pale, but inanimate camel; an UNBORN CAMEL! Shocking!

As I came nearer, I observed how others partook of the meat from this tiny creature. They were very deft in stripping small pieces of flesh from the little animal and dipping it in *berere*, an Ethiopian hot sauce. I'm sorry to say that I can't describe how it tasted. I don't think it had a distinct flavor; however, I do remember that it was not unappetizing. (I was probably still marginally traumatized by eating unborn camel. My taste buds had possibly gone into shock!)

Incidentally, the unborn camel was only the first of many unusual delicacies that I had the occasion to eat—in Ethiopia and other countries. I should quickly add that some of these foods were not easy to eat, which is an understatement! Back in the 1950s in Ethiopia, and in subsequent countries where I travelled, it would have been unthinkable not to try the food of the host nation. It would have been offensive. Consequently, attempts were always made to eat the food that was served and to gallantly try to come up with something positive to say about what had been consumed. On some occasions, this was truly very difficult to do!

Other interesting foods that I've had the dubious pleasure of eating were: fried grasshopper, rat, beetle, live octopus, an assortment of live fish, chicken claws, dog, blood pudding, alligator, ostrich, warthog, kudu (antelope), and an assortment of other African game—to name but a few.

Still, having eaten exotic foods in many countries of the world— nothing made more of an impression than the UNBORN CAMEL served at the Haile Selassie University in Addis Ababa!

Chapter 7

ADDIS ABABA TO DJIBOUTI AND YEMEN (ADEN)

I had lived in Ethiopia for a few years and had heard intriguing stories of Yemen—a remote and mysterious country. I was eager to visit this exotic place, so two friends and I decided to make a trip into this relatively unknown country. After a planning meeting we decided to take the train down to Djibouti—which was also a "less traveled country"—and then fly over to Aden (Yemen).

We arrived at the train station a little early because we knew there were no seat assignments and there might be difficulty in getting a seat. There was already a sizable group of people, and shortly after our arrival a train pulled in. Everyone hustled to the train to get a good seat. We followed suit and fortunately were successful. However, we barely got our belongings stowed when the train started slowly moving away from the station—much sooner than was scheduled. Locals on the train became agitated, started yelling, collecting their many belongings and quickly disembarking from the train—which meant jumping off! We had no choice but to follow suit—we also jumped! Luckily, all three of us landed on our feet—safely on *terra firma*. It was apparent that the train we had been on was only moving to another track; consequently, when the train started moving we assumed we were on the correct train. At that time in Ethiopia there was only one railway in the entire country. The situation is the same today, although the Chinese are presently building a new track.

Within a few minutes of our jump another train arrived; it was necessary to participate in the same "free-for-all" to secure seats on the new train. We were quite aware that we would be spending the entire night on the train, and we wanted to avoid sitting on the floor in the aisle, which we knew often happened. Fortunately, there were three of us and we were able to push, shove and secure seats: my companions got two seats side by side, facing me on the other side. The wood seats were without padding, seat backs were "straight up," and the seat where your bum resided was far, far too narrow. All of these inconveniences made for considerable discomfort. Fortunately, my seat-mate was a nine year old girl, shy and well-behaved. I enjoyed teaching her some American words and attempted to add Ethiopian words to my vocabulary. There were no other *ferenjis* (foreigners) in our train car and frankly, it was unlikely there were any foreigners in the entire train.

We had been told we would be traveling with as many "four-legged creatures" as there were *homo sapiens*—and this was nearly true. It was not a surprise to see on the train baskets with live chickens, a few goats, a dog, a small pig—even live fish in water containers, and other unidentified "critters". We fully realized that we were in for a noisy and uncomfortable 14-16 hour ride, depending on scheduled and unscheduled stops and the condition of the railroad tracks. We didn't get much sleep that night on that long, long train ride. But we were young, ready for adventure and prepared to enjoy ourselves no matter what!

Weary and worn, we finally arrived in Djibouti, a French port city situated on the Tadjoura Gulf. It was, and still is, the capital and largest city in the country, with most of the inhabitants being Islamic. We arrived well before lunch and, since our plane didn't leave Djibouti until later in the day, we decided to take a walk around the main part of town; which we did, in oppressive heat. We saw a fountain with a cascade of water, where we could sit and cool off before going to the airport. We took advantage of it.

During the time we were sitting there, some adorable little kids came up to talk to us. They wanted to practice their English. As we were talking and being entertained by these "cuties" we were also distracted. Yes—one of our cameras was "slicked"! We had fallen for the "ploy" that is used the world over on unsuspecting visitors.

Flying into Aden, Yemen, a British colony until 1963, was an extraordinary experience. The Ethiopian Airlines pilot circled the city and we were able to observe that it was divided into two distinct districts: the old Walled City, and the newer City on the outskirts. The Walled City was situated in the crater of a dormant volcano. Buildings were nestled deep, deep down within the black ash of the volcano. It was an extraordinary sight!

After circling several times, we landed and found a taxi to take us to the newer part of the city to hotel accommodations. We settled into a western-type hotel which had the barest of necessities. We stashed our belongings and then walked around in that general area, careful to return to the hotel before nightfall. We had been advised before leaving for this remote country to be extremely careful in all our activities. Yemen was certainly not as dangerous as it is now, but it was not a country where we ever felt comfortable. A year or so before our visit, a United States Aid for International Development (USAID) employee working in Ethiopia had visited the country and, in the public square, had seen a native's hand chopped off at the wrist. That native had been caught stealing. This was his punishment, which was traditional—and still is in various countries of the world.

There were not many *ferenjis* seen during our entire visit, and the ones we met were mostly British. They were not as friendly as one might expect. We asked the hotel manager to find us someone that was trustworthy to accompany us into the Old City and stay with us during our visit. There were no city or country tours at that time. The following day, an Arab in native garb escorted us into the crater. He was not especially friendly, but spoke English relatively well. More importantly, we trusted him.

The interior of the Walled City was a chaotic mass of activity. I would describe it as a gigantic bazaar that bombarded the senses with a host of unusual sights and sounds. Hundreds of locals in stalls, huts and old shacks were selling their wares: clothing, bedding, fabrics, kitchen utensils, tools, coffee, spices, wheat, dried foods, limited fruit, a meat market (rather horrifying), fish, and a variety of other merchandise. Mingled in with all of this were live goats, donkeys, camels, mules, cows, and other farm animals. And then there were mounds of chat. (*Chat is a narcotic leaf imported from Ethiopia to other countries in the region. It was a known fact that in the early years of Ethiopian Airlines, transportation of chat to neighboring countries was a major factor in its financial survival.*)

We spent several hours in the market without buying anything of substance, and left the bazaar feeling like we'd walked out of an exotic movie set. I think we didn't feel comfortable in Yemen because it was a very different culture from other cultures more familiar to us. It was rather like "traveling back in time" to Medieval times. Knowledge of some traditions, such as amputating the limbs of thieves, stoning of women and other shocking laws added to our discomfort.

Merchants in the market were not as friendly as in most other marketplaces we visited, and not seeing any women except those fully covered in their "*hijabs*" only added to the mystery of the market. I've had the opportunity to visit numerous markets and bazaars in various countries. I can truthfully say that I was more uncomfortable in the Aden market than in any other, with the possible exception of Peshawar, in Pakistan.

On the third day we left Aden and flew back to Addis Ababa, having experienced a few days of uncertainty in a Godforsaken country. We didn't regret making the trip, but not one of us *ever* intended to make a return trip to Aden—or to Djibouti.

Chapter 8

A Car In Oklahoma:
A "Royal Car" In Ethiopia

My parents called me in the spring of 1952 to tell me that they were going to take a contract with Point Four (United States Aid Development) and move to Ethiopia. I immediately asked, "When do we leave?" They responded that I would not be going with them. They wanted me to finish college. I was a sophomore studying piano at the University of Oklahoma at that time. I was terribly disappointed, but was somewhat pacified when they said that they would be leaving the family car with me when they left. At that time few students had cars on campus. I was elated! I was going to have my own wheels on campus—what a deal!

A few months later I had another phone call; not a good one. My parents called to say they had been advised that it was necessary to take to Ethiopia all food they would need for at least one YEAR! Can you imagine? That would include such items as sugar, flour, salt and pepper, coffee, tea, ketchup, mayonnaise, mustard, canned items—and a thousand other commodities that were needed for daily food consumption. Unfortunately, my parents didn't have much money, so they had to sell "my" car for the money needed to buy the necessary food provisions. Talk about disappointment! I remained in college for another two years and had to hoof it around campus—without wheels. I didn't know it at the time, but rather than having use of a car on campus—I was to receive "something else" upon graduation that was far more valuable and that changed my life forever.

After graduation, I got on my first plane *ever* and took off for Addis Ababa, Ethiopia—spending time via the Big Apple and several weeks in Europe. Shortly after I arrived in Addis, I made arrangements with some Americans that were leaving country to purchase their small Volkswagen for my use. Before taking possession of that car, I needed to borrow my parent's car. They had bought a white four-door Chevrolet upon arrival in Addis two years earlier. It was used on occasion; but their Land Rover was the primary means of transportation.

When I left the house one beautiful morning, it was another gorgeous day in Addis. Every day in Addis was lovely, with blue, blue, skies and temperatures at 75 Fahrenheit year around. My Dad told me that I might have an unexpected surprise when I drove down the street, so I should be prepared. I had no idea what he was referring to, but before driving a short distance from the house, the "surprise" became apparent. As I drove down the street, in my big, white, four-door Chevy, native Ethiopians began throwing themselves on the ground or bowing deeply as I approached. Amazing!

I didn't know it when I left home that morning, but it was the custom to bow or prostrate one's self on the ground any time His Majesty's car approached—as a matter of great respect. Since there were very few cars on the roads, my large, white, four-door Chevy was mistaken for one of His Majesty's cars. Imagine!

Actually, the Emperor often rode standing in an open-air jeep, with two lions sitting on the car seat behind him. He had another enormous car, a limousine from England, which was used on more formal occasions and during the rainy season. My drive in the long, white, Chevy was rather unsettling, but a fun escapade!

Happily, I was able to take possession of my own small Volkswagen within a couple weeks. When driving it, no one ever bowed or threw themselves on the "terra firma" when *I* passed by!

Chapter 9

THE HYENA MAN

Oklahoma State University (OSU), under the auspices of Point Four (now known as United States Aid International Development), was established in 1954 in Alemaya, Ethiopia. It is now referred to as Harayama. Eleven students were enrolled and were offered a range of classes in related disciplines of agriculture. They subsequently graduated in 1958, with a Bachelor of Science degree in General Agriculture. His Imperial Majesty, Haile Selassie, attended that graduation and formally inaugurated the campus at that time. Alemaya still has the distinction as one of the oldest universities in Ethiopia and presently has an enrollment of nearly 8,000. My father was an employee of the Point Four project during those years; consequently, I had the occasion to visit the campus several times. One of those visits holds a special memory for me.

Two friends and I made the trip over to the eastern highlands of Ethiopia where Harare, a walled city, is located. It was a short distance from the Alemaya campus. (Harare, at this time, is said to be the fourth most Holy City in the Islamic world. In 2000 it was recognized as one of UNESCO's World Heritage sites. UNESCO is the United Nations Educational, Scientific and Cultural Organization.) After spending time with OSU friends and visiting the huge outdoor market—and other intriguing places—we decided to make a visit to the relatively unknown "hyena man" later that night.

The hyena man lived on the edge of the city near a gigantic garbage heap where many hyenas hung out. He fed the wild hyenas by hand every night around midnight. It was near that time when we made our way out to the hyena man's *tukel*. (A *tukel* is an Ethiopian house. It is circular, made of dung and mud, with only one entrance and no windows. All *tukels* are one room, and this one was perhaps 30 feet in diameter with a small hole in the ceiling for ventilation purposes.)

On this night a small fire had been built in the middle of the room. When we arrived we were taken into the smoke-filled *tukel* and gestured to sit down on a dirt floor, which we did. The hyena man then picked up a bone from a nearby handful of assorted raw meats and bones. He went to the entrance of the *tukel* and called out in the darkness to the hyenas: "korrr, korrr, korrr." Within a few minutes there appeared out of the black night, a fierce, scruffy and vicious looking hyena. The hyena slowly entered the room—coming in only a few feet—and with its savage jaws clamped down on some raw meat and slinked away into the dark night. Then, the hyena man gestured to indicate that one of us could feed a hyena. Both my companions, David and Pete declined—but the "adventurer" in me took hold and I nodded. "Yes!"

I remained sitting on the ground and was given a bone from a large animal, perhaps three feet long. I carefully took the end of the bone. The hyena man went again to the entrance and called out: "korrr, korrr, korrr." Soon a wild-looking hyena appeared in the doorway. The animal cautiously entered and approached us—and the bone which I held. Keeping as far from the hyena as possible, I extended my arm away from my body and held the long bone at the tip. I leaned slightly forward to tempt the animal, watching… watching… watching intently. Suddenly, the wild animal lurched forward, seized the bone in its terrifying jaws and darted out of the *tukel*. It was a jaw-dropping experience!

We left the hyena man standing in the doorway of his *tukel*. Leaving the stinking garbage heap with the wild hyenas, we stole into the night. We knew that we had just had a haunting encounter in deepest, darkest Africa; one that would never be forgotten.

Chapter 10

EMASCULATION IN
THE DANAKIL DESERT

Occasionally, OSU employees combined professional trips with recreational ones. Professional research in various disciplines such as agronomy, agriculture, water development, livestock, mapping and geography all were required for the Point Four mission. However, once the work was done we were usually ready for a leisurely exploit. The trip to the Danakil Desert was one of those explorations.

After several days of hard driving, most of which was on dirt roads or no roads at all, we finally pitched our tents on the edge of the Danakil Desert; a dry, barren, and seemingly desolate place. This desert is one of the lowest and hottest places on earth, sometimes reaching temperatures as high as 124 degrees Fahrenheit. In this particular desert, salt deposits and lava lakes that were formed thousands of years ago still exist.

We had driven 16 hours that day, so while we unloaded our gear from the Land-Rovers, our evening meal was being prepared over a campfire that had been built. Before our simple dinner was served, we shared our favorite time of the day when traveling in the bush: Happy Hour! On this particularly eerie night there was a feeling of uneasiness in camp. Why? It was because we knew of the horrifying tribal rite which was peculiar to the Danakil desert. We were also acutely aware that we were in an area of Ethiopia that few *ferenji* traveled.

It was an enigmatic setting. As we were enjoying Happy Hour and preparing our tents for the night, a few natives came quietly to watch what the *ferenji* were doing. We could barely see them as they stood in the twilight, perhaps 15-20 yards away. Each leaned on a tall spear—with one foot propped up on the other leg. As dusk turned to darkness, there was little light except from the campfire and kerosene lamps which had been placed in each of our three tents. All components of this desert adventure made for a bizarre experience—with sinister overtones. After dinner, the imbibing continued and "yarns" from previous trips into the bush became more exaggerated as the night darkened. But one "yarn" was truth—not fiction—and it was enjoyed more by the women than the men.

In this region of Ethiopia, it was known that when a young man became "of age" and needed to prove himself for the responsibilities of manhood, he had to accomplish many feats. He was no longer a child, so he carried a fierce-looking knife at all times. Without a doubt, the most dangerous and horrifying undertaking was to raid another tribe, capture a male tribesman—and then emasculate him! The testicles were brought back to his own tribe as evidence of his savage coup. The testicles were final proof that he was ready for the responsibilities of manhood.

It was also a known fact that, in years past, victims had always been Ethiopian natives, usually from neighboring tribes. But in recent months a different story had been circulating, and had been *verified*. The story was about how an Italian driver of a lorry had been caught in the Danakil area—and was a victim of this appalling procedure. We sat around the campfire that night and elaborated on this gruesome native ritual, and became more and more consumed with the mystique of the night.

Finally, it was time to turn in. We each went to our tents, which formed a triangle around the campfire. There were three tents: two couples (the Murrays and the Kalings) each had their tents, and we three Skinners had our tent. My cot was at the back of the tent and my parents' cots were at the front.

Several hours after we retired—in the still of the night—there were blood-curdling screams, yelling and wailing from one of the tents. It brought the fear of God to us! My mother, being nearest to the entrance to the tent, grabbed a flashlight and peered outside. Not seeing anything except the embers of the fire, she quickly left the tent going in the direction of the commotion. By the time the rest of us got out of our tents, the delirious and crazed sounds had been replaced by sobbing—intense sobbing.

Huddled together near the campfire with arms around each other were Charlotte and Murray. Both were near hysteria—especially Murray. What happened?

It seems that Charlotte had awakened, shook Murray to say that she was going out to the back of the tent to relieve herself. She asked her big-boned, 6'3" husband to be "on watch." When she returned, her husband, not fully awake, jumped on her and started furiously beating her up. He thought that the natives were after him! Startled, she screamed bloody murder and he began yelling hysterically. When the rest of us finally appeared they had come to realize that natives had not invaded our camp to castrate Murray—or anyone! We stood around the embers of the campfire until everyone calmed down—particularly the Murrays.

Few jokes were ever made of this bizarre event. We were too close to the reality of this horrendous ritual to joke about it. It was simply one of those mysteries of life in the African bush.

Finally, with some trepidation, we returned to our tents. No one got much sleep the remainder of night. It truly was a night to remember and it still evokes an incredible memory of our strange experience on the Danakil desert.

Chapter 11

OVERLAND ADVENTURES: NAIROBI TO ADDIS ABABA

It was the summer of 1958 when I made one of the most memorable trips of my lifetime. We were three (David, Pete and I) and had just completed six weeks of an amazing adventure of driving through several counties of East Africa, to include Kenya, Uganda, Tanganyika, Rhodesia, the Belgian Congo, and Somalia. It was now time to start the very challenging road trip back from Nairobi to Addis Ababa, which was not attempted often in the mid-50s.

To accomplish this we had to travel through the Northern Frontier of Kenya, the oldest frontier in Africa—and reportedly the most dangerous. It was necessary to travel in caravan because of *shifters* (bandits) and the inhospitable and remote territory we would traverse. We had previously applied for required special passes from the British District Office in Nairobi and had received permission to make this grueling trip.

There were three vehicles in the caravan—all Land-Rovers. A total of seven of us were making the trip. We met the day before our departure at the famous Stanley Hotel in Nairobi to assess what provisions we would need: water, food, shovels, picks, extra tires, car-jacks, ropes, chains, a compass, and other miscellaneous gear. We would be traveling with two British couples, each in their own Land-Rovers, and the three of us in ours. One of the couples was

Leslie Casbon and his wife, whom I knew in Addis Ababa. Leslie was the consummate frontiersman, having lived in Africa for a number of years. He was a natural-born leader, having proven repeatedly to have exceptional survival skills in the "bush." We had great confidence in his ability to lead us safely back to Addis Ababa. Incidentally, Leslie's wife was related to the famous British suffragette, Sylvia Pankhurst, who had close ties to Emperor Haile Selassie and his family.

Addis Ababa, the capital city of Ethiopia, was from 700 to 1000 miles from Nairobi, depending on road conditions and the routing of our trip. We had been advised to take a compass with the expectation that it would be needed. At our planning session the day before we left, we came up with several important rules for the trip. The most important one was that we would travel close to each other—always trying to keep within eyesight of the other vehicles.

We left the next morning at the break of day. Leslie's vehicle was in front; our vehicle was second, simply because we were the youngest and least experienced. I was to do all the driving, which probably made them nervous. Finally, the other British couple brought up the rear. Driving out of Nairobi was not difficult, but as we traveled in a northeastern direction we observed that road conditions were deteriorating. There were fewer private vehicles, maybe a bus or two, and considerably more natives on foot—with a mix of donkeys, goats, camels, and other livestock. We drove hard that day, leaving paved roads for dirt and gravel. Fortunately, we got through that stretch of territory without incident, making camp before dark.

On the second day, we got another early start. We soon realized that the physical features of the land had significantly changed from a landscape of some vegetation and greenery to a more semi-arid terrain. There were fewer vehicles on the road that day, but more livestock and natives. The road was becoming more punishing.

Natives were not as friendly as back in the Nairobi region. Around four or five o'clock on that second day we could see in the distance a British outpost which was our destination for that day. As we came nearer we could see a large building on an escarpment with a few smaller buildings scattered around. All the buildings were one story and the architecture was similar to Native American adobe structures. Soldiers in uniform, natives, a great number of camels, and other livestock, were milling around as we came nearer the outpost.

At the gate to the compound we were met by a British officer and a couple of his aides. The District Office in Nairobi had radioed them to expect us. We were then escorted to the administration office to sign papers that verified we had arrived safely without any difficulty, and would be leaving the next morning for Addis Ababa. After signing the needed documentation, they took us to our quarters for the night, which were on the open-air roof of the administration building. Cots had been set up for us, as had been table and chairs, where our evening and breakfast meals were served.

As our evening meal was being served, we were told to expect a surprise around sunset and that we would have choice seats from the top of the roof. We couldn't imagine what was to transpire, but were certainly more than a little curious. We were facing the West and could see the beginning of a beautiful desert sunset with the British Union Jack flying on a flag pole not far in the distance.

Without warning, there was a great deal of commotion below us—camels, soldiers, rifles, a bugler, natives in traditional local garb, a few stray goats, and various other livestock. It was a chaotic swarm of man and beast. Looking down from the roof we observed that soldiers were mounting camels and lining them up in a straight line facing the sunset and the flag.

Suddenly, a single bugle sounded as the Union Jack was slowly lowered—with everyone standing at attention. After the flag was folded and delivered to the officer in charge, all hell broke loose! Buglers sounded the military cadence; soldiers fired volleys into the sunset, and at least twenty camels with soldiers astride, raced fiercely into the sunset, yelling, shrieking, and screaming at the top of their voices! It truly was like a scene out of "Lawrence of Arabia"—an unforgettable spectacle!

At that time in history, and earlier, similar military rituals took place at outposts of the British Empire. I'm under the assumption that the riflemen, perhaps ten of them, fired the volleys and were members of the notorious Kings Rifles. They were known worldwide and had often served on the Northern Frontier. We had much to discuss that night about the events of the day, especially about the wild ritual we had just witnessed. We eventually climbed into our cots expecting a quiet and peaceful night in the desert. That was not to be. Yet another event would challenge our senses.

In the not too far distance we heard a mixture of sounds drifting over the desert; sounds we were not accustomed to. We heard the grunting of camels, braying of donkeys, bleating of goats and sheep, even some bells and a gong—and a profusion of other unidentified sounds. The sounds were coming from the area where the camel-riding soldiers had raced.

We got up from our cots to take a look at what we were hearing. Looking across the desert we saw numerous small bonfires, literally hundreds and hundreds of camels and a hodgepodge of other animals. They were all gathered at a water well, having come from various parts of the desert to drink. They also filled large, leather water bags which would be needed for their travels. We were told that they came for water every night from across the desert. Approximately 1,000 animals came that night—most of them camels.

On the third day we left for what we knew would be a couple of very rough days, primarily because of treacherous road conditions. *Shifters* were still a problem but they were now on the "back burner"; nevertheless, we made the decision for our caravan to travel closer together. As we continued to the Northeast the landscape again changed significantly. We were seeing less desert; more greenery and vegetation and more natives and livestock. We had definitely left the desert. We think we crossed the border into Ethiopia near Moyles, but were not sure as there were no authorities around to check our visas and passes.

Road conditions continued to deteriorate—at times nearly impassable. On several occasions we had to get out of our vehicles with picks and shovels to move objects, or do whatever was necessary so we could pass. This was a continual necessity over the next two days. We were in increasingly dense foliage, narrower roads, and the much-dreaded mud-mud-mud. We had anticipated the mud because we were traveling during the rainy season in Ethiopia.

Fortunately, our caravan did not see a drop of rain on our entire voyage. But the rains had come with a vengeance and damaged the already near-nonexistent roads and moved on. We continued on through what seemed like mounds and rivers of mud, which on occasion came up to the running-boards of our vehicles. Out came the shovels again.

Near the end of that first day of mud, we came across a family of missionaries (Mom, Dad and two young children) in a large flatbed truck. They had been stuck in the mud for nearly two weeks! Their food provisions were a little low, but their water situation had become critical. We hoped we could give them some assistance to get them out of their unfortunate situation. With our Land-Rovers, ropes, chains, shovels, and other necessary equipment, we were able to pull them out of the mud. We gave them a few jugs of water and some food provisions and saw them on their way. It was relieving and very rewarding to see them drive off to their mission in the "bush".

⌇⌇⌇

After the missionaries left, we had one more harrowing driving challenge. We had left most of the mud behind, but then came to roads that had deep, deep ruts—evidently made by big lorry trucks that sometimes traveled these roads. The ruts were so deep that we had to drive the Land Rover so that it straddled them; the wheels on the left at the edge of the dense jungle and the wheels on the right along the ridge in the middle of the road. It was extremely hazardous!

Another time, on an incline, it was necessary for riders in each vehicle to get out and place their hands on the upper part of the Land Rovers for support. Our efforts prevented the vehicle from tipping over on its side. This was an equally risky and dangerous action!

Eventually we came out of the muddy area into dryer land. We were feeling good about our trip, knowing that the worst was behind us. We had met the challenges of the trip so far without any serious difficulty. More importantly, we would probably make it back to Addis Ababa the following night. We were eager to get home. We were tired and muddy, but content that night as we set up camp.

The following morning we followed a *quasi*-road for several hours, but before long we had to rely on the compass—which we had anticipated. Fortunately, Leslie, our lead driver had relied on compasses in previous travels. We were confident that we wouldn't be "lost forever."

The last day was the least eventful of our trip, but we did come across a subterranean well. Intriguing, to say the least! When peering down from the surface of the ground into the well, we could see that the interior was not in a smooth vertical line. For balance, natives that were working the well stood on angular rock surfaces that jutted from the earth. Because of the darkness we were able to see only two natives from the top, but were told that there were usually six or seven men below the surface. They worked hours at a time, passing up water in leather pouches to their co-workers at the top. This water would subsequently be taken to villages for its people and livestock. We tried, unsuccessfully, to find out how long this water well had been used. They replied: "We don't know. The well has always been here."

After leaving the wells we ultimately found the one and only major road; the compass was no longer needed. As we drove down the road we knew we'd make our destination before sundown. We were excited! We finally arrived, still tired, unwashed, dirty and muddy. Yet, we were full of memories of having successfully driven from Nairobi to Addis Ababa, a journey that—at that time—not many *ferenji* had ever attempted.

Chapter 12

KING TUT'S TOMB—THEN AND NOW

It was the summer of 1955. I had just graduated from the University of Oklahoma and was on my way to Addis Ababa, Ethiopia, with my mother. We had spent six weeks in Europe and were eagerly looking forward to the last leg of our trip, which included Luxor, the Valley of the Kings, and the famed King Tut's Tomb.

After spending several days in mysterious Cairo, we took an overnight train to Luxor. The train had no air-conditioning or circulation of any kind! With the sand and dust it was necessary to keep the window cracked open to have air to sustain us. The heat was intense. It often reaches 120 degrees Fahrenheit in Egypt. With the window open, the sand and dust that permeated our train's sleeping compartment was stifling—just dreadful. We arrived in Luxor the following morning after a miserable night, completely saturated with this pale, brown, loose substance known as sand. Awful!

After taking in the wonders of Luxor and Karnak, we left for King Tut's tomb which is located in the Valley of the Kings. We stayed in an enormous old English hotel, the Winter Garden, and to our delight it had limited air-conditioning. Few other hotel guests were seen in the lobby or dining room. The hotel had made all arrangements for our trip to the tomb which was across the river: The Nile River. We got a good night's sleep that first night as our accommodations were much more desirable than the sandy, hot train.

We awoke the next morning excited about the prospect of finally seeing this historical and celebrated world attraction. We met our guide in the lobby and walked to the Nile's riverbank. There we found an ancient, small boat with a boatman sitting in it. There were no other tourists joining us for the tour, which was a little surprising. However, we had already observed that there were few other tourists, so we should not have been shocked at being the only ones going on the tour.

The guide, my mother and I stepped into the boat; Mother and I were seated in the middle, the tour guide sat at the front, and the boatman was behind us. The river was not particularly swift, yet our boat didn't exactly inspire confidence for crossing to the other side, which was approximately one mile away. The boatman rowed at a rather slow continual pace until we reached the distant shore. It was a non-eventful crossing, but certainly scenic.

On the shoreline we could see a one-horse buggy and driver waiting for us on a sand-and-pebble beach. Strangely, there were no people on the beach; no souvenir stands, no young children, nothing except our horse and buggy. It was almost uncanny. We disembarked, got into the buggy and took off at a slow trot on an unpaved trail up to the area of the tomb. Surprisingly, upon arrival at the tomb area we observed only a few people. Most of them were old men sitting around in the limited shade.

In the 50s there was no electricity in the tomb area, no refreshment stands, no souvenir stands, no water fountains, not even any bathroom facilities that I remember. There were none of the conveniences that tourists expect today. My mother and I were each given a candle and a flashlight to be used in various sections of the darkened pathway to the tomb. The guide also carried a flashlight and candle as we descended toward the tomb. We were surprised at how often we had to use our candle during our slog down the passageway.

We descended 16 steps—precisely 16 steps. After 31 years of looking for King Tut's tomb, a famous British Egyptologist finally discovered it 1922. At that time the entrance of 16 steps was totally blocked. This was evidently done to discourage bandits from entering the tomb. Most other tombs in the Valley of the Kings had been already robbed.

After clearing the stones and rubble from the area the Egyptologist counted exactly 16 steps. Once he determined that he had finally discovered the tomb, he immediately filled in the passageway until security measures could be implemented to protect his discovery. It was not until several years later that the passageway was permanently opened.

Before entering a long, tunnel-like pathway leading down to the tomb, we had been told that we would have to stoop low, and even crawl short distances before arriving at our destination. With our instructions and the guide leading the way, it was necessary to do exactly as we had been instructed. After crawling for some distance balancing our candles, we finally reached the antechamber. Crawling around on hands and knees was definitely not easy—even for the young. There were four main rooms in the underground area, but because of the darkness I only remember entering two rooms: the antechamber and the burial chamber. The antechamber and treasury rooms are the only ones directly connected to the interior where King Tut is entombed. We were in near-total darkness; consequently, were unable to determine exactly where we were being led. Nonetheless, I do remember crouching in the antechamber room at the end of the pathway. We knew we were close to our final goal—King Tut's tomb.

Fortunately, after we entered the burial chamber we were able to stand upright—a welcome relief! Upon entering the chamber I was struck by the smallness of the room, the low ceiling, and of course, the magnificent gold coffin of King Tutankhamun (Tut). There were paintings on the walls, but because of lack of light we could see only small segments of the murals and their vivid colors when our guide held his light to them.

The guide pointed out the more significant paintings and explained their historical and artistic significance. The tomb, in the center of the room, was elevated to display the king's mummy more effectively. Despite the lack of sufficient light, we were dazzled by the solid gold sarcophagus, the famed mask with its semi-precious inlaid stones, and other unimaginable treasures that adorned the room. It was everything we had hoped to experience.

Our return trip was uneventful except for a side trip that was not expected. The guide suggested that if we agreed we'd make a detour on the river when returning to the hotel. He told us it would be spectacular, even though unplanned. He assured us that it would take less than an hour and would not be dangerous. Of course, we agreed.

The boatman turned the boat downstream and not long thereafter we could see two magnificent sandstone statues standing in the middle of the river in the distance. Absolutely astonishing! We approached within about 200 yards to take a closer look. Oh my, the guide was certainly accurate, the statues were truly stunning!

I returned to Luxor and to King Tut's tomb years later. After waiting at a large terminal building in Luxor, I crossed the river in a modern air-conditioned ship that held hundreds of passengers. We entered a terminal building on the other side. We were greeted by tour guides and escorted onto a gigantic air-conditioned bus which took us on a wide, paved road up to the tomb area. Upon seeing the changes that had taken place in this vicinity, I was dumbfounded—absolutely shocked!

A few modern buildings were scattered around near the entrance to the tomb. There were bathroom facilities, water fountains, vendor stalls and souvenir shops for mementos. There were young and old sellers circulating in the crowds pushing their wares, there were a few beggars, there were private and public vehicles, there were crowds of people, and yes, there were a few horse and buggies. The atmosphere, regrettably, was like a "three ring circus." However, the transformation that I most appreciated was the entrance to the tomb and the interior of the tomb chamber—it was amazing!

The 16 steps that led down to the tomb were wider than the original pathway, solid as a rock and decorated attractively. There were sturdy hand rails, and best of all, there were electric lights in the tomb area. Being able to see entire walls of colorful murals depicting the history of Egypt and the life-story of Tutankhamun was a genuine history lesson. The dazzling splendor of the famed King Tut resting in his solid gold tomb and the celebrated gold mask that had been placed over his head and shoulders was an indescribable vision. Sensational! Breathtaking! Historians of today indicate that the mask most likely represents a very true likeness of the king.

At that time, I had never heard of the Abu Simbel Temples, but several years later I saw in a publication that in 1968 two magnificent temples were being moved from the water to what is now their resting place in the Abu Simbel village in southern Egypt. In viewing publications and photos of the temples I was convinced that they were the two massive temples we had seen standing in the Nile River near the Valley of Kings. They were moved due to the rising water and construction of the Aswan Dam. It was a necessity. The temples are now listed on the UNESCO's List of World Heritage Sites to see.

But alas, on my return trip to the area years later, the two massive temples were still in standing. However, there was a great difference. They were standing on dry land—dry as a bone!

In retrospect, I prefer my first visit. It was more authentic. It hadn't been assaulted by the inevitable modern changes that are often necessary to tempt the "maddening crowds" away from the comfort of their homes and their own familiar cultures.

PART II

EXOTIC TREKS THROUGH ASIA

Chapter 13

THE ROOF OF THE WORLD: PAKISTAN TO CHINA

In 1987, the Karakoram Highway opened, going from Rawalpindi, Pakistan, up to the Khunjerab Pass in China, the world's highest border. It is considered the "Roof of the World" and the road leading to it is the highest paved international road in the world. It is often listed in current travel literature as the Eighth Wonder of the World. It took several decades to construct; because it is so narrow and precarious many lives were lost and it is still considered an extraordinary engineering accomplishment. It navigates one of several ancient Silk Roads, traveling through the Gilgit, Swat, and Hunza Valleys up to the Chinese border. These names have become familiar in recent years because of the conflict in that part of the world.

It was the summer of 1988 when two friends and I decided that we would travel to the Roof of the World during our summer vacation. We flew into Islamabad and stayed with a U.S. Colonel, his wife and a magnificent bulldog whose name was Balzaak (and who looked remarkably like Winston Churchill). Our host, the Colonel was a friend of one of my traveling companions.

On the morning of our second day, we did some sightseeing in Islamabad and bought some basic necessities for our ensuing trip. In the afternoon we were driven to Peshawar to meet our driver, at which time we made final preparations for our journey. Our driver was a tall, scruffy, unfriendly Pakistani; was blind in one eye and wore a black patch over that eye. He also had intense body odor, which we were to discover was prevalent in the confines of our car for the entire trip. The car we would be traveling in can only be described as an old jalopy.

Neither car nor driver inspired confidence! But the driver did speak reasonable English which we knew would be critical for this journey. We had reservations about his reliability, but since our host had recommended him as trustworthy and capable we had no recourse but to accept him as our driver. We were told after we left Pakistan that the Colonel often used him for smuggling U.S. arms into Afghanistan. WOW!

The following morning we left in our jalopy, with our one-eyed driver, feeling somewhat apprehensive. Our ascent that day took us up through the Gilgit Valley, a lovely green area with sheep, goats, and other livestock grazing peacefully in the meadows. We spent the night at the Gilgit Hotel, which proved to be the most "comfortable" hotel of our entire trip.

We continued our climb up through the Hunza Valley, with the Hunza River paralleling the road much of the way. The river was a swirling, angry, dirty body of water that varied in width and swiftness as it crisscrossed the deep, rocky canyons. It would ultimately present great danger to us before we returned to Islamabad. Fortunately, there were not many vehicles on the road going in either direction. In places only one vehicle could pass at a time. Because of the narrowness of the road, there was a lineup of vehicles wanting to take their turn to continue on their way. Luckily, we didn't have long to wait. Even more alarming were the unprotected road edges on one side of the road, with drops of thousands of feet. On the other side were solid rock facades of the mountains.

We continued on up through a more desolate and remote region into the Swat Valley. (This region is where the now-famous Malala Yousafzai lived before her assault. She is the young Pakistani activist who fought for her right to an education, *as a girl*. Malala had refused to be silenced when the Taliban took control of the Swat Valley. She was only 15 years old at the time and was shot in the head while riding a bus home from school. She subsequently won the Nobel Peace Prize becoming the youngest recipient ever of that prestigious award.)

Our accommodations on the Karakoram highway were extremely rustic. Rarely would the motel have both water and electricity, but it usually had one or the other. Nevertheless, we survived. After all, we were on an adventure of unknown challenges and were psyched-up to face whatever obstacles came our way.

One motel merits special attention. Let me introduce *The Marco Polo*. It was situated within a few hours of the summit and had neither water nor electricity. Our tiny rooms were cramped, windowless, with dirt floors and with one single item in the room—a filthy bed. It was disgusting. The bathroom facility was even worse. We had anticipated these inconveniences and adapted reasonably well, except for *my* sleeping situation. My friends shared the other room and had to adapt to less dire circumstances.

My mattress was revolting. It was stained; made of coarse, prickly, rough horsehair and had no bed sheet. It did have a foul-smelling, grimy, heavy blanket to use as a cover. I was totally convinced that both the nasty mattress and blanket had all types of parasites and vermin. I was appalled. Moreover, there was a horrendous odor in the room. I thought it might be a dead rat, which would not be uncommon.

After a brief time of trying to adapt to this unacceptable sleeping situation, I finally moved outside and slept under the stars. A good move! The stars were incredibly bright that night and I felt that if my arm was just a little longer I could reach out and touch one of those shining stars. I did not sleep well that night. It was cold and that itchy, foul-smelling blanket with the hard-as-nails pillow made for a sleepless and intensely uncomfortable night. Furthermore, I was somewhat wary and feeling unsafe with the two or three creepy men who ran the hotel. We did not see any women during our stay there. Still, I survived the night, and never doubted that my decision to move out of that despicable room to sleep under the stars was a good move.

We left early the next morning, knowing that we were not far from our destination—the ROOF OF THE WORLD! The topography on that last day was much like I would imagine the surface of the moon; stark, dry, barren, completely inhospitable. One had a sense of nothingness like a vacuum. Much to our surprise, there in the center of all this nothingness was a gas pump where we filled the tank.

We continued our ascent. Up, up, up—and finally reached the Khunjerab Pass—the Roof of the World! The spectacular panoramic view took my breath away. It was awe-inspiring, stunning and wondrous! What made it so spectacular, so unforgettable? We were viewing the Hindu Kush, Himalayan and Karakoram Mountain ranges—the highest concentration of mountain peaks to be found *anywhere on the face of the earth.*

This unbelievable vista encompasses over 30 mountain peaks that rise to over 20,000 feet, and eight of those peaks were above 26,000 feet! Each of us turned, ever so slowly around in a full circle to digest the magnificence of the mountains. We even tried to count the peaks. After a few minutes of total silence—which for me reflected a profound spiritual experience—we quietly walked up a hill. About 50 yards away was a rustic sign indicating that we were, without question, at the Roof of the World. A Chinese couple was taking pictures of each other in front of the sign. They seemed friendly. Even though we couldn't communicate, we smiled often at each other and pointed to the majestic mountains. No words were needed.

We spent less than a half-hour at the summit before starting our descent. We were at an altitude of over 15,000 feet and it was beginning to take a toll of us. Besides, it was necessary to get back to Gilgit and on to Islamabad to take a plane that flew only once a week to our next destination—Srinagar (Kashmir) India.

That descent from the pinnacle of the world is where we faced a significant challenge—an adventure that could have been fatal.

You'd think our adventures were over at this time. They were absolutely not! There was another hazard further down the road which could have been tragic.

After taking another view of the sweeping spectacular mountain ranges, we started our descent. On the second day we had an unfortunate incident, which later snowballed into a monumental adventure. Our one-eyed driver ran over a small rock in the road. A small rock, yes, but it did great damage to the old jalopy. It ruptured the gas tank and fuel spilled out over the roadway into the crevices. It was apparent that our days with the jalopy and driver had ended.

We had not been pleased with our good-for-nothing driver. He drove like a "bat out of hell" even with our constant complaining. We had become resigned to his recklessness knowing quite well that we were being treated as inferiors, as women in his country and countries all over the world were often treated (and still are).

The segment of the road where we hit the rock was on a rather high hill and not well-traveled. We had seen few other vehicles. We were in a dilemma as to what to do about our unfortunate circumstances, but after talking with our less-than-satisfactory driver, we decided to push the car down the road. We hoped that it would get enough momentum to make it to the river, which we could see in the distance with a few small structures nearby.

So our ambitious undertaking began. We pushed and pushed; jumped in to coast for a short distance, then repeated our efforts—again and again. Fortunately, before we were totally exhausted, a truck with several members of the Pakistani Corp of Engineers came upon us and offered to tow us down the road. Out came a rope which was secured to the jalopy's front bumper and off we trailed behind the Engineers truck down the hill toward the bridge.

The buildings that we had seen from a distance were the Corp of Engineers camp. Upon arrival, an Engineer hastened to tell us that they would not be allowed to take us any further down the hill. Thus, our driver consulted with on-site mechanics to see if our car could be repaired. Sadly, no such luck! As a result, we had no options except to try to hitchhike back to civilization. Oh my!

With considerable hesitation, we did what was needed. That was to attempt to flag down any vehicle coming down from the summit. With luck, before too much time had elapsed, a Pakistani General in a military jeep with his son and a friend stopped and picked up the three of us. (Our good-for-nothing driver stayed behind.)

After several hours of making our descent in the General's jeep, we went around a bend at the top of a hill and literally ran into the end of what had been a mammoth landslide. The slide covered the entire road for perhaps 100 yards and extended on down into the river. The dust was so thick from the falling rocks and debris that we could hardly see the front of the jeep. The General got out of the jeep, walked down to the troops and engineers that were working near the landslide and water's edge to assess the damage. We watched from the jeep, which was perched on a hill. We wondered how on earth we'd make it back to Gilgit in time for our flight to Islamabad. After a brief time, the General returned and said his decision had been made. He would try to ford the river around the landslide and pick up the road at the other end of the slide.

The General was aware of our need to get back to Islamabad. His decision to ford the raging river was not to be taken lightly as the powerful, swirling river appeared to be an extremely dangerous option. As passengers that had been rescued by the General, we had no option except to "go with it."

The General drove cautiously into the angry, ferocious river. Water started immediately seeping into the jeep—getting higher and higher. Our situation was becoming precarious as it appeared that the General has lost control and that we would soon be swept down the spiraling river. One of my friends, sitting in the front seat, started screaming with fright; the other, sitting in the back with me, was alarmed but was taking it in stride. On the other hand, I was attempting to take pictures of the rushing water that was sweep-ing us down the river and coming higher and higher into the jeep. It was a perilous and dangerous episode! The General eventually gained control of the vehicle, and we made it to the other end of the landslide. Whew!

On reaching the other side, we were able to get back on the road. We soon picked up more military personnel which rode with us back to Gilgit where we caught the short flight to Islamabad. That ride to Gilgit with the General and other troops made for a cramped and crowded vehicle. Since there were few seats in the jeep, we sat on the floor with the troops for the next 4-5 hours. Not comfortable!

Happily, we were able to catch that short flight to Islamabad and arrived back at the Colonel's house around midnight. We were finally in a safe and clean haven. We were totally exhausted, but thankful that we had been rescued by the General—and had not been swept down the raging river in the jeep.

The following night a dinner party was given for us, at which several Pakistani Generals were present. There was some serious talk about the landslide, but mostly it was a fun evening during which we got teased about our adventure. The host had a player-piano, and much of the evening was spent around the piano enjoying the music. One of the Generals was an accomplished pianist, who knew some popular American songs, as did the other Generals. With a few libations under our belts we sang lustily well into the night.

The following day we left for a week on the legendary, storybook houseboats of Kashmir. But, my, oh my! We boarded the plane having survived a grueling adventure on our amazing journey to the Roof of the World.

Above: The Pass (Roof of the World) is the world's highest border. The view from the Pass is the highest concentration of peaks to be found any place on the face of the earth.

Below: Military personnel working on the massive landslide between the summit and Gilgit.

Above: Filling up the gas tank near the Roof of the World.
Said to be, at that time, the highest "filling station" on earth.

Below: Pakistani women and children who were as
curious about us as we were of them.

Chapter 14

A Journey To Sikkim

Aknock on the door one night in the fall of 1972 brought with it an interesting invitation. Two girlfriends invited me to accompany them on a trip—and an *illegal* one at that! The destination was Sikkim. Americans were not allowed into the country at that time. This unique opportunity occurred because one of the gals had recently transferred to Korea from Japan. She had been working with a Japanese travel agent who was arranging a tour for her and two others into Sikkim. I was one of those lucky two. Without hesitation, I accepted. What an opportunity!

We left Seoul on December 22, flew into Haneda, Japan where we met Mike, the travel agent, and received some of the official papers that would be needed for the trip. The next day we flew into Calcutta where we spent the night.

The following day we visited the Calcutta Travel Agency. We were expected to receive air tickets for the flight up to Darjeeling, the entry city to Sikkim. We had unfortunate news when we arrived at the travel agency. It seems that all flights and trains in the entire country were on strike. This was, and still is, a normal state of affairs in India. The agents expressed their regret stating that we would not be able to go to Darjeeling or to Sikkim because of the strike. After the three of us conferred, we stated that we were definitely going to continue our journey—by car! The agents were horrified at the thought that three young American women would even consider such a trip. We prevailed, noting that we had come a long way to visit Sikkim, and insisted that we should be able to continue on. Subsequently, we requested that they find a suitable driver for our trip, which they did. Regardless, they were not happy about it.

The next morning our driver arrived and we started on our long and dangerous 16-hour trip. We took only our carry-on luggage, leaving larger suitcases in the hotel. Our driver for the trip was not a cautious driver and seemed to think that if he kept one hand blowing the horn—for every single mile of our trip—then every living creature should get out of our way. Fortunately for us—they did!

We drove through hordes and hordes of people and animals (cows, goats, sheep, dogs, a camel or two, and numerous other four-legged creatures). All were sharing space on the road with buses, cars, lorries, bicycles, and our own speeding vehicle. The driver, the locals, the animals—ALL seemed completely unaware of the dangers of mechanized vehicles! It was a hazardous 16-hour drive! We made a couple of rest stops along the way, and also enjoyed a box lunch that our hotel had fortunately prepared for our trip.

We arrived in Darjeeling and went directly to the appropriate government office to get the necessary documents for continuing on to Sikkim. Again, those government agents were surprised to see us, assuming we would not have been able to make it to Darjeeling because of the strike. They were also reluctant to let us continue. Nevertheless, we were resolute and after another hassle convinced them that we would not be turned away. We finally succeeded and were assigned a driver and Land Rover for the rest of our trip.

After leaving that office, the driver took us to our hotel. Unexpectedly, but to our great pleasure, it was the world famous Windermere Hotel, situated high in the hills of Darjeeling at an altitude of over 5,000 feet. This hotel is where Hope Cook, a New York socialite, met and later married the King of Sikkim. To this day it remains on the list of the Top Ten Hotels in all of India.

Our driver picked us up early the next morning and we started up to Sikkim, which was considered a "State" of India. This trip would have been very difficult for travelers affected by heights. Sikkim's altitude is over 8,000 feet and it is nestled high, high up in the beautiful eastern Himalayan range. None of us had any difficulties with the high altitudes we were traveling. I attribute that to our slow ascent from Calcutta up to Darjeeling and on to Sikkim.

We were told that few tourists, of any nationality, ever visited the kingdom at that time. The road we traveled was under construction, and on occasion we had to remove rocks and other debris to proceed. It was not an easy ride, but in spite of the road construction it was an enjoyable one. The road traversed lush, dense vegetation and tea plantations as far as we could see. Happily we were able to get glimpses of the magnificent Himalayan range every now and then. We met only a few other vehicles on the road, and saw few people. We did observe, however, that although this was a poor region, it did not reflect the abject poverty and misery of Calcutta and other parts of India.

Upon arrival, we checked into the only western hotel in the country. It had what appeared to be about a dozen rooms. The hotel was adequate, but a surprising fact was that we were *not* given keys to our rooms. We were told by the manager "not to worry—no danger!" Moreover, we became aware that we were the only people that had stayed in the hotel since December 6th. Amazing! It was Christmas Eve 1972.

After leaving our belongings in our room we immediately left for Gangtok, the capital city and site of the Royal Palace. The palace was a wood, three-story structure; not large, but attractive with exterior walls painted in bright colors. There were several acres of grounds surrounding the palace, but no fence or wall for protection. Unfortunately, the palace was closed that day due to a national holiday.

We were told that the King, Queen and children had left for the Christmas holidays— each to separate locations. (Incidentally, I had written for an audience with the Queen, knowing quite well that it would not be granted but thought it would be fun to try. It was not to be. The Queen and her children had left a few days earlier for New York.)

We had been told by locals that the Queen was not at all popular with the Sikkimese. She did not attempt to learn the language or customs of the country and on several occasions had her wealthy friends flown in from New York and Paris for lavish parties to which few Sikkimese were invited. (I've always thought that perhaps when she married the King, she assumed she'd be living the same privileged lifestyle as did Princess Grace of Monaco with Prince Rainier. That was certainly not the case. The King and Queen eventually divorced. She returned to New York with the children; he died an alcoholic.)

During the time we wandered around the palace grounds, we were lucky enough to watch a national archery tournament. Archery is as much of a passion with the Sikkimese as baseball and football is to Americans. It was a colorful and fun competition to view! Nevertheless, other than the archery games, we did not see as many people as we had hoped during that day or the next. Unfortunate.

The town of Gangtok would hardly qualify as a town. Some streets were paved, others were not. The limited commercial district consisted of long, low, dilapidated buildings in various states of repair. We found only one small shop that was open—perhaps 12 feet by 12 feet—with sod floors. It was filthy dirty but had a few items of interest to buy. I couldn't resist, so I bought a small, intricately carved wood piece for the wall, and a favorite acquisition of mine—the "Dragon Ring."

Through ensuing years, that ring and other unique pieces of jewelry collected in my travels have generated some great conversations. Best of all, years later I discovered that the ring's small stone in the mouth of the Dragon was a genuine pearl. I paid only $5 for the ring!

We retired to our hotel that night, feeling just a little disappointed at what we had seen that day. I'm not sure exactly what we had anticipated; perhaps a more ostentatious palace and certainly we wanted to see more locals.

The next morning, a knock came at the door and to our surprise the manager entered our room—without being invited. He announced to us, his pajama-clad guests, "Breakfast is being served in the dining room." We hastened to the dining room to find a very lavish and typical British breakfast served at our table. There were several appetizing courses—for only the three of us. Most enjoyable!

Our second day we drove up to Ramptek, a monastery. Other than a few monks, there were again few locals to be seen—disappointing. The monastery was situated on a plateau with several long buildings facing each other, rather barren with few trees or vegetation. Between the buildings was a covered open area. Monks and others met there to visit, meditate, drink tea (probably Darjeeling), and pass the time of day. Fortunately, there was a friendly monk who kindly led us through most of the monastery. He related to us a little history of his country and of that famous abbey. Ramptek continues to be the largest community of monks in the land and is the repository for sacred items and relics. Moreover, a "College for Institution of Higher Buddhist Studies" was, and still is, on the same premises.

The next day we left Sikkim for an uneventful ride back to Darjeeling, staying again at the famous Windermere Hotel. The following morning, we started on the same arduous 16-hour trip back to Calcutta with the same heavy-handed driver on the horn. I've always thought that the three of us gals set some sort of "distinguished record" on the car ride to and from Calcutta. Why? Because not one of us used a restroom during those SIXTEEN HOUR drives! I defy anyone to find three adult American women who can go sixteen hours without a "rest stop!"

Still, our adventures weren't over. We had heard before arriving in Calcutta that there had been a citywide, hotel-employee strike. The hotel where we were to stay—and where we left our luggage—was no exception. When we arrived at the Hotel we were "locked out." We couldn't get in the front gate. With some "tall-talking," we finally entered, got our luggage and moved to another hotel.

We left Calcutta the next morning for Kathmandu, Nepal—our next exotic destination.

Chapter 15

TORAJALAND: DEATH AND BONES

Christmas of 1981, I made a trip to Jakarta, Indonesia, to visit my brother. After a few days with him I flew to the remote island of Torajaland. It is the Regency of South Sulawesi Province, formerly known as Celebes. After finding suitable accommodations, the hotel provided me with a driver. He also served as my guide while I explored this unfamiliar and isolated country.

Torajaland was, and still is, an exotic "off-the-beaten-track" destination. In 1981, only 12,000 tourists visited this country. Today it remains a remote destination, but it is becoming more of a "not-to-be-missed" target for the adventuresome. It was unknown to the world until Dutch missionaries discovered it early in 1900. It was subsequently used as a source of slave-trade.

Torajaland is a country of complex blends of ancestor and animistic worship regarding the belief that natural objects have souls. Rituals for the dead are colorful, preplanned festivals that pave the way for the soul's entry into the hereafter. These ceremonies are not morbid. They are considered to be "going-away celebrations" for loved ones.

Torajaland is also renowned for its ancestral houses. Structures are boat-shaped and stand on high wooden piles. Split-bamboo roofs shaped like curved arches reaching for the sky make for a very unusual exterior. The first impression I had of these unique structures was that the house was about to "take off in flight to the heavens." Paintings and carvings on the exteriors of houses were in bright colors of red, black and orange, and were usually of animals and plants. These were symbols of considerable significance in the culture. Ownership of water buffaloes and buffalo horns hanging on the exterior of the house indicated great stature and wealth in the community.

When I visited, a Torajaland village was composed of the ancestral houses of extended families. These were the social and cultural centers of the island. A typical village had as many houses as there were extended family members. Houses were clustered together within eyesight of each other, and each family member was expected to participate in every element of family life. It's my belief that this is still true. Total commitment to the family is expected. If one does not cooperate, the individual is highly ostracized, and in rare cases is dismissed from the family unit.

Funeral rites are extremely important social events and depending on the wealth of the deceased—very elaborate and expensive. Sometimes as many as 1,000 guests attend the funeral ceremony. The events last many days, even months, and for noblemen—longer. Massive funds are needed for a wealthy person's ceremony and years are often spent in preparation for the celebration. In addition to water buffalos, pigs also indicate the wealth of the deceased. For a powerful aristocrat, herds of buffalo and pigs are slaughtered by machetes at the climax of the death feast. The belief is that the deceased need the buffalos and pigs to journey with them to their afterlife.

When a death occurs, the body is embalmed, wrapped in cloth and placed in a coffin. It is then laid in a separate room in the house, or under the house in a protected area. It remains there until extensive funeral preparations can be made. This is necessary to enable family and friends to come from afar— even from off the island. Consequently, preparations are lengthy and costly.

The cadavers are cared for in their homes by family members until the funeral takes place. I was fortunate to visit several homes of recently deceased members. One was a middle-aged man who was kept in a coffin under the house at ground level. (Farm animals, too, are also often kept under the houses, or nearby.) The other corpse I viewed was laid out in a separate room on the second floor of the living area and was lying on a plank. I was told that she was a grandmother in her 60s. The room was immaculate with very little in it except the board where her body was laid and a chair. She was not wrapped in a cloth, but was fully clothed. She appeared to me as if she had just come in to lie down for a rest. Family members often came to "visit" with Grandmother until her burial ceremony. The belief was that her soul was still present and would be until after the funeral rites. Hence, she was still a significant and respected member of the family.

There are several methods of burial in the Torajaland culture. In preparation for the funeral ceremony the body is wrapped in cloth and placed in a coffin. It is then "buried" in a cave below ground level or hung over a cliff. Both underground and cliff caves have spaces large enough to hold possessions of the deceased which might be needed in the afterlife. For the very wealthy, graves are carved out of the cliffs. They are huge chambers that are not only for an individual's bones and possessions but also for the bones of that person's ancestors.

Preparation of cliff graves was a very expensive undertaking and often required months to make ready. After the burial ceremony, life-sized wooden images of the dead were created and then covered with clothes that the deceased might have worn. Often, even hats were placed on their heads. These standing images were then situated two, three, or four stories above ground. They were positioned to face outward—looking over their holdings. Once a year family members replaced the clothes on the effigies with new apparel.

I was fortunate to have the opportunity to go into several of the ancestral caves. These caves were of different sizes and shapes and at different levels from the ground. There was no conformity in their size or configuration. To enter, I had to stoop low. Once inside, there were times when it was necessary to crawl between the chambers of the caves. A few bones were scattered around on the floor but most were in stacks, carefully piled near the walls.

The caves were dry and clean except for a dust-like substance hanging in the air. There was sufficient light to see in most of them, but a few were so dark that I elected not to enter. In each cave there were hundreds and hundreds of bones of every size and shape. These were bones of ancestors from previous generations.

When a baby or infant died, a small coffin with the tiny body was hung with ropes on poles extending from cliffs or trees. The coffin remained suspended until the ropes rotted and they fell to the ground. Bones were then collected and taken to the family ancestral cave. Mercifully, I saw only a few tiny coffins suspended from trees. A rope suspending one of the coffins was rotting. I thought that it wouldn't be long before the coffin would fall to the ground. The bones would then be taken to be united with bones of ancestors that had preceded the baby in death.

I stayed two nights in the country, so had only one full day of touring. I was able to see only a small part of Torajaland—which is a country also known for its stunning, untouched beauty. Even so, I've always been thankful that I had the opportunity visit this relatively unknown island. I saw for myself its famous ancestral houses, and left with greater knowledge of its strange and unique funeral rites.

Above: Ancestral houses of Torajaland.
Most houses are boat-shaped and appear ready to "take off in flight."

Below: Typical villages of the ancestral houses are
usually clustered together for families and relatives.

Above: The deceased are usually placed with other deceased members of the family, and are always faced outward looking over the holdings of the family.

Below: Slaughtering Buffalo and the climax of a death feast.

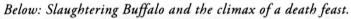

Above: Life-sized images of the very wealthy are carved of wood and placed on cliffs several stories above ground.

Below: Images are covered with clothing, sometimes even hats. Clothing is changed every year.

Water buffalo horns on houses indicate the wealth at stature of the deceased.

Chapter 16

MYSTICAL TIBET

The year was 1998 and Tibet had recently opened its borders to foreign travelers. For several years, Tibet had been one of those countries high on my list of places to visit. I immediately started planning a trip for a small group of friends that were as eager as I was to visit this ancient and unknown country. At that time I had a small "moonlighting" job with Cathay Pacific Airlines as a travel agent arranging tours to many destinations, especially those in Asia.

Tibet is often referred to as the "Third Pole of the Earth" and also as the "Roof of the World" because of its unique topography. It has five mountain ranges of over 26,000 feet and most mountains in the country are over 22,000 feet. We were not only keen to see the magnificence of the mountains, but also to learn more about this unexplored country.

Our group of seven boarded the plane for our first destination, Kathmandu in Nepal, one of my favorite countries. Our purpose was not only to enjoy some sightseeing, but also to slowly acclimate to higher altitudes. Kathmandu, an ancient and mysterious city, has an altitude of 5000 feet. Lhasa, our first destination in Tibet, is at 13,000 feet.

It was a known fact that flying up from Chengdu, China, to Lhasa was not encouraged, but at that time it was the standard routing. The drastic change in the air, in such a brief time, often put individuals at risk for mountain (or altitude) sickness. In ensuing years tourists have either taken the train or driven up from Chengdu, making it easier to adjust to the thin air.

When arranging this trip, I was fortunately aware of great disappointments of the first travelers going to Tibet due to altitude problems. The previous year, eight friends of mine had made the trip to Lhasa. Three of the eight were so sick because of the high altitude that they never left their hotel room for their entire seven-day trip!

We stayed in Kathmandu only for a few days before leaving for Tibet. After three days we flew on up to Lhasa, the capital city of Tibet. We went through tight passport control and met our Chinese guide, who had flown up from Chengdu earlier that day. Unfortunately, he was already having altitude problems. Regrettably, our guide never fully recuperated and had health issues the entire trip.

After completing necessary documentation for entrance to the country, we were taken to one of the few western hotels in Lhasa, the Holiday Inn—an unfortunate name, to my way of thinking. I don't know if the hotel was connected with the world-wide Holiday Inn® hotel chain. Perhaps it was just a name the Tibetans came up with to attract tourists, but I thought it was inappropriate. Happily, the name was changed several years later to reflect the ethnicity of the country.

When checking in at the hotel reception desk, we were strongly advised to walk very slowly back to our rooms, not to exert ourselves, and to rest for several hours before even considering venturing out. We complied with their request. Our rooms were standard fare, but with one exception—each room had a canister of oxygen. Happily, none of us had the need for oxygen until later in the trip when we were at a considerably higher altitude.

After several hours we were antsy and wanted to do some exploring so we ventured out—with the guide in tow, of course! The little time we had on that first day was spent exploring the area close to our hotel; nevertheless, a couple of us were able to sneak away from our guide and enjoy a little freedom. We realized this would probably not be possible in the days to come. Throughout our trip, we were usually within eyesight of our guide, so when given a measure of freedom we scattered—making it difficult for him to keep track of all six of us. It became something of a fun game with us. We called it: "hide from the guide, hide from the guide." In reality, our guide was a very pleasant young Chinese man who enjoyed our group of women and we enjoyed him. He said it was the first time he had ever "escorted" a group of women—let alone American women—on a tour of Tibet. We also had a great deal of sympathy for his continuing health difficulties.

The following day our formal tour of Tibet began. There were three main tourist attractions in Lhasa: the Potala Palace, the Jokhang Temple and the Barkhor District. The morning after our arrival we visited the spectacular Potala Palace. It is a huge Buddhist monastery that sits on a hilltop overlooking the town. It dates back to the Seventh Century, has over 1000 rooms, is 13 stories high and is certainly the focal point of Lhasa. It's where the Dalai Lama lived in his early years. It is not used much as a monastery at this time, but remains important as a destination for devout Tibetan Buddhists and other pilgrims.

We were able to go through numerous rooms of the palace, each room being more enigmatic than the next. Rooms were dimly lit by candles; incense and burning yak butter permeated the air. Colorful Buddhist statues of gods and goddesses of various sizes and reposes looked down upon us. Donations of food and money had been left in front of various statues and on altars. Ceiling and wall coverings of exquisite silks of various ages and conditions reflected the history and teachings of Buddhism. There were numerous monks circulating throughout the palace. Most were oblivious of us.

We had been cautioned not to engage in any conversations that touched on sensitive political problems that divided the Tibetans and Chinese. The Potala Palace, the Jokhang Temple and most Tibetan monasteries had been infiltrated for years by Chinese posing as Tibetan monks. China had invaded Tibet in 1950.

There was little communication between the monks and us. It's doubtful that even a handful of either Chinese or Tibetans spoke any English. Before our trip, we had been told not to bring any images of the Dalai Lama into the country. If caught we would face serious repercussions. Sadly, several in our group ignored instructions and concealed pictures of the Dalai Lama in the inner-soles of their shoes. Thankfully, no one was caught.

After visiting the Potala Palace, our next major site to visit was the Jokhang Temple. The temple sits in the middle of the old section of Lhasa. It's not as large as the palace, but is more active in terms of Buddhist worship. As was the case in the palace, sounds of chanting were heard throughout the building as worshippers prayed. Some instructional classes were in session and were being taught by experienced monks. My general impression was that the Potala Palace was more of a destination for pilgrims, whereas the Jokhang Temple was more of a school for monks.

Large prayer wheels circled the Jokhang Temple which is common in most Buddhist monasteries in Tibet, Nepal, and other countries of the world. Those who are devout walk around these places of worship in a clockwise direction spinning large prayer wheels as they pray. Many were also seen fingering prayer beads. The very devout can be seen prostrating themselves on the ground every few yards as they circle the monastery saying their prayers. It is said that it often takes hours and hours to complete a circle of this monastery in that distinct manner. It must have been exhausting.

Exiting from the temple we found that we were in the Barkhor district and market. This area surrounds the temple and is a place where political demonstration had taken place in the past. It is also a commercial district where we found souvenir shops and stalls selling a great variety of commodities. There was a range of items to be purchased: Buddhist religious items, jewelry (lots of turquoise and coral), Tibetan carpets, prayer rugs, precious wools, shawls, garments made of yak and cashmere, and a multitude of other goods. Fortunately for us, prices were unbelievably low in all the places we visited.

Tibetan women also were always present in front of our hotel with their collections of merchandise for bargaining or sale. Happily, their domain was truly a bargaining paradise for merchants and tourists alike. We were able to trade our old clothes for items of interest—and of worth. I traded a pair of old tennis shoes which was on their "much wanted list." The shoes were traded for a chunk of turquoise as big as an egg. Fantastic!

On our last day, as was our custom when visiting other developing countries, we left gifts. This time, for the women we left an assortment of our clothes. As we had found in other locations, the clothes were much appreciated.

After a few days in the Lhasa vicinity, we left for other regions of interest. Shigatse was our next destination. It is considerably higher than Lhasa. At 16,000 thousand feet it is one of the world's highest cities and the home of one of the most massive monasteries in the country, if not the world. Regrettably, by the time we arrived in Shigatse the altitude was beginning to take a toll on our group. One was experiencing a little dizziness, another a headache and several of us were taking in great gulps of air. Nonetheless, two of us were able to walk up a short hill, perhaps 25 yards away, to the highest point. Everywhere you looked hundreds and hundreds of prayer petitions and colorful flags were tied to poles, and also placed on or under rocks. These petitions are requests for something "hoped for" in their lives.

In Shigatse we settled into a hotel with only the essential necessities, but it was adequate for the night. However, in the middle of the night came a trauma for which I was not prepared. My roommate, an Asian-American, had known before leaving for Tibet that she had difficulties with high altitudes. A recent altitude problem had been in Denver, Colorado which was considerably lower than any place in all of Tibet. She had taken precautions for this trip by taking a medication, often used by those climbing the highest of mountains.

On the other hand, I had been advised by a military doctor on the base where I worked not to take any medications. He advised me that when taking a medication, people seldom know they are at risk—until the problem is critical. Unfortunately, that is exactly what occurred. After receiving medical attention, she was quickly diagnosed as having pulmonary embolism—which validated the advice my doctor had given me.

It was about 5 a.m. when I was awakened by my roommate. She was having great difficulty in breathing. I immediately left to find our guide for help. None of the hotel employees spoke English. The guide quickly determined that medical help was indeed needed. He called for the driver and we left for a clinic not far from the hotel.

The clinic was disgusting. The few medical personnel we encountered were in filthy scrubs, a couple of mangy dogs were lying in the hall and absolutely nothing looked hygienic. Unquestionably, there were no signs of any attempts of cleanliness or sanitation any-where. It was appalling!

A doctor was waiting for us. He examined my friend, looked up in alarm and exclaimed that we had to get her back down to Lhasa and out of the country—ASAP. We were startled to find that we had no recourse except to do as we were advised.

Nevertheless, logistics of our situation had to be considered. Two of us were returning to Lhasa, and the others would remain to enable them to continue their tour. They would return to Lhasa sev-eral days later. A driver that was willing to take us back to Lhasa in his car was finally located. We were given a canvas oxygen container about the size of a pillow. Lisa was told to breathe from it every hour on the return trip.

Before we could leave, another problem surfaced. It was our guide. It had been his responsibility to watch closely over all of us the entire tour and we were now separating. Consequently, he had a dilemma. Fortunately, he was quickly able to contact the head office in Lhasa to ask what he should do. The decision was made for him to accompany us back down to Lhasa, and leave the others with the driver and van to finish their tour. That decision was made, in part, because of his health.

For the entire trip, our guide had continued having difficulty adjusting to the thin air. Altitude problems can vary—from head-aches, to dizziness, to diarrhea, to vomiting, to a host of other dis-agreeable stages of misery.

It was near midday when all the decisions had finally been made. My roommate, the guide, the driver, and I started the harrowing trip back to Lhasa. It was one of the most dangerous car trips I'd ever experienced. The road was a loose gravel winding road, with hairpin curves, and drops of thousands of feet on the sides—with no barriers. It was a hair-raising ride! Rather than driving at a reasonable speed, the driver seemed to me like he competing for the Indy 500. (Perhaps he was concerned about the patient, but I sincerely doubt it.) When the others returned to Lhasa several days later, we were told that they made the trip in a little over eight hours. It took us five!

We arrived back at the Holiday Inn, went immediately to our room and called for the hotel doctor, who surprisingly (in those days), was a female. She arrived within minutes. A doctor was on call at any time of the day or night in our hotel. After a quick exam she indicated that she did not think the situation was so serious that Lisa would need to leave the country. Instead, she recommended we go to the hospital for another assessment—for a second opinion.

We were walking up the steps of the hospital when we were approached by a Tibetan woman who said to us, "You don't know me, but I work in the tour office and I am the person who is responsible for your Tibetan trip." She continued on to say that there was another option to consider before going into the hospital. She recommended that we go to a very small clinic on the edge of the city to get another opinion, and if that doctor recommended that it was necessary to leave the country—then we should go—quickly!

She went on to explain that there was quite a sham going on with the hospital. It seemed that foreigners who were admitted to the hospital got very good care, but were required to stay for a lengthy time. When they were finally dismissed (usually after a week or more), the bill they were presented was exorbitant! The situation had become so blatantly obvious that some embassies were checking to see if any of their citizens had been admitted. If they were, close surveillance was kept on their progress. When necessary, the patient was taken from the hospital to the embassy, remaining there until their departure from the country. It didn't take us long to decide to try the option of the clinic.

After our decision was made we were then taken by the travel office representative to the suggested clinic. The clinic was a room about eight by ten feet, furnished with a cot-like bed, a small desk, a light bulb hanging from the ceiling, and a tall, large, metal oxygen container. There were no windows in the room; only a door which opened from the street directly into the room. It was dirty. It was grimy. It was ghastly. It didn't inspire confidence. Still, even after seeing the condition of the clinic and talking with yet another female doctor, Lisa decided to risk it.

She made an appointment for the following day for eight hours of oxygen to be followed by bed rest. Lisa was a remarkably strong young woman and a great admirer of the Dalai Lama. She had assisted me in arranging this trip and was primarily focused on visiting the Summer Palace, which was the last residence of the Dalai Lama before he went into exile. She was insistent about staying in the country and finishing the tour. Incidentally, my friend was born in San Francisco to a Korean father and Chinese mother. She spoke both languages and several more. Her Mandarin was very useful throughout our trip—certainly during her illness.

Over the next couple of days, we went to the clinic and she took oxygen for eight hours. During those hours I sat in the chair and visited with Lisa, talked with the doctor, read, and wandered the neighborhood to observe the people and surroundings.

The Tibetan travel representative checked in on Lisa several times a day—even bringing us food and water. Lisa and I had several interesting political conversations with her. She had been living at home when the Chinese forcibly entered their house and removed her father. He had never returned or been heard from since. As a result, she had become bitter, but her bitterness inspired compassion for others who were not in power. For us, that translated into her action to protect us from being taken advantage of by the hospital scam.

At noon on the third day, Lisa was strong enough to be discharged and we joined the others who had returned from Shigatse the night before.

The next day we returned to the Jokhang Temple and Barkhor Market area, site of the political demonstrations where recent deaths had occurred. This was our last opportunity to enjoy the famous, sacred Buddhist Jokhang Temple and to buy souvenirs. There were fantastic bargains in the country and we did our very best to "stimulate the economy." I bought some lovely coral jewelry; others purchased wools, shawls, embroideries, scrolls, paintings, and a multitude of other handicrafts.

❧

The following day we visited the Summer Palace. I had noticed on previous days of our trip, Ann (a member of our party) often lagged behind when we visited the monasteries and temples. She was usually the last to leave these sites of Buddhist worship. I didn't give it much thought, being aware that she was Buddhist. However, on the final day of our tour, in the last room we visited, she was really lagging behind—more than usual. The rest of us had already started toward the van. I was beginning to wonder why she was taking so long, but within a few minutes she joined us. She was obviously shaken, flustered and disturbed.

We hurriedly got into the van and she shared with us a curious encounter she had just experienced. She related that as she was leaving that last room, she was approached by a monk who was behaving rather strangely—glancing over his shoulder, looking around the room to see if other monks were in the room. He undoubtedly considered himself in danger. He then asked in broken English, if she would take a letter of great importance out of the country when she left Tibet. She didn't know what to do, being apprehensive of the political situation in the country. Regardless, Ann agreed!

As she was telling us about her encounter, we encouraged her to open the letter. To be expected, it was not written in English, but in Tibetan. We planned to spend one night in Kathmandu on our return trip. Thus, we decided that we'd take it to the Tibetan Refugee Center and have it translated when we returned to Kathmandu the following day.

The next day after arriving in Kathmandu, we immediately went to the Refugee Center, not knowing if our unusual request would be accepted. Fortunately, they were eager to help us. It was a long and tedious effort, simply because of the limited English ability of the translators and the length of the letter—four pages long. The contents of the letter were shocking! It told of demonstrations that had taken place in the Jokhang Barkhor area several weeks before our visit. Several deaths had reportedly occurred at that time.

There had been no account of this uprising, or of the deaths, in any known publication. The monks had prepared this letter with the hope that it would be taken out of the country and news of the killings be made known to the western world. After the letter was translated our plan of action was for Ann to take the letter back to her husband for appropriate action. He worked closely with the U.S. Embassy.

By sheer coincidence, Ann's husband was one of the highest ranking American civilians working in Korea. He worked with the U.S. Embassy and Military on all issues related to North Korea and other countries in Southeast Asia. Prior to this position, he had served with the Peace Corps in Korea. He spoke Hangul (the language of Korea) and several other languages. His primary responsibility was to read any and all publications that could be obtained concerning subversive countries—especially North Korea. The letter that was given to Ann by the monk at the Summer Palace was subsequently delivered to her husband. He then included it in the daily diplomatic mail pouch from Korea to Washington, D.C.

Weeks later, I read in the base newspaper, *The Stars and Stripes*, about the rioting that had taken place in the Jokhang Temple/Barkhor Market area and the resulting deaths.

In retrospect, I think Ann's bizarre experience was likely more than a coincidence. Perhaps it was a plot that Ann's husband had preconceived. Undoubtedly, because of his high-ranking position with the U.S. Government, he most likely had knowledge of the rioting and perhaps even had contacts within Tibet. It further explains some of Ann's peculiar behaviors on our tour. She had not kept up with the rest of us on visits to various monasteries and temples and a few other incidents that left us curious.

Potala Palace. A huge seventeenth century Buddhist monastery that overlooks Lhasa.
It is the focal point of the city and where the Dalai Lama resided.

A group of great gals on 'top' of the magnificent Potala Palace looking over the city of Lhasa.

The colorful and exotic Barkhor District and market. Also a site of politica demonstrations.

The authoress at Shigatse. At 16,000 feet, one of the highest cities in the world. Prayer petitions and colorful flags are tied to the poles or placed under rocks requesting "something hoped for."

Interior room of a Buddhist monastery
with a gigantic Buddha and a monk.

A monk, a yak, and a gal.

Chapter 17

ELEPHANTS, RHINOS AND
THE TIGER TOPS LODGE—OH MY!

I had ridden elephants before. But, this adventure on an elephant was like no other before—or since...

We had flown in a small plane from Kathmandu to the Bharatpur airport and were *en route* to the famous Tiger Tops Jungle Lodge in the Chitwan National Park in Nepal. Flight attendants had alerted us to expect a rough landing due to the unevenness of the dirt landing field. We were apprehensive! After being advised by the attendants we tightened our seat belts, bent over and braced ourselves for the landing. We prepared for the worst. Thank goodness it was not nearly as hair-raising and dangerous as we anticipated.

Looking out through the small window of the plane we immediately saw that there were three elephants kneeling in a row at the edge of the landing strip. What an unexpected sight to see! We could hardly wait to disembark from the plane. We had been told that elephants would be waiting to carry us to the lodge, but kneeling in a row at the airstrip—how exciting! A few passengers with us on the plane elected to go to the lodge by Land Rover rather than by elephants. I always wondered if they didn't regret their decision not to ride the elephants.

Before being taken over to the pachyderms, we had to first go through passport control. After disembarking from the plane we walked over to a long table positioned at the edge of the airfield to get our passports stamped. This was the terminal: there was no building, no walls, and no roof. Nothing except a table with two men sitting there with a few papers scattered about and the stamp pads for our passports.

After getting our passports stamped, a representative from Tiger Tops greeted us and taking our backpacks he led us over to the three elephants that were still kneeling. There were six of us and each elephant would carry only two. The representative introduced all of us to our own *mahout* (the driver, trainer and elephant keeper). He explained that the elephants would remain kneeling until after the plane departed so it would not frighten them when taking off. While waiting for the plane to leave we took some pictures of the kneeling pachyderms, milled around them, giggled a lot, and gingerly touched them—with the encouragement of the *mahouts*. It was decided that each elephant should have a name. We gave our elephant the name "Jumbo." Not very original, but what name would have been better?

After the plane took off we paired up and were taken to the specific elephant we were to ride. A short wooden ladder of sorts was resting against the side of the elephant. The *mahout* had already taken his place on the neck of the elephant with his *gord* (stick) which was used to control the elephant. I hated seeing him prod the elephant with the *gord* which had a metal hook on it, but knew it was a necessary evil in those days. It was not pleasant to see.

The rep from the lodge helped each of us as we awkwardly climbed up the rickety wooden ladder. It was a little scary but, with moans and groans and more nervous giggles, we eventually made it up to a box-like platform placed on the back of our Jumbo. This is where we were to sit for the next three-hour safari through the swamps and jungle to the well-known Tiger Tops Lodge. Exciting!

I shared the ride with my friend Angela who had recently joined the Department of Defense Dependents School program and had been assigned to teach in Korea, like me. She had lived all her life in Manhattan and had traveled extensively, but never to Asia. She was somewhat anxious about this jungle adventure. Nevertheless, Angela proved to be a great traveling buddy; a happy soul who laughed a lot and was very adaptable.

Before the rep left with the others in the Land Rover, he told us that we should be looking for all sorts of wildlife on our journey; monkeys, tigers, birds, some rhinos, and possibly a crocodile or two might be sighted on our ride to the lodge. We giggled nervously, but were eager to start the safari. When the elephant arose from the ground, it took some strength and balance not to fall off or out of the box-platform where we were perched. There were some squeals and moaning, but fortunately, no one fell off.

As we set off for the lodge, each of our three pachyderms went in a different directions. We were told that a rhino had been seen between the airport and the lodge, and it was hoped that there would be a sighting. Our chances were better if we separated. It took us nearly the full three hours to arrive at our destination, but what a storybook adventure it was. We went through swamps, crossed a river, went uphill and down, over short and tall grasses (elephant grass), and through dense jungle with our Jumbo swaying back and forth as he walked.

Angela and I giggled so much and so loud that our *mahout* continually tried to "shush" us because of the possibility of scaring away any wildlife. As we lumbered through the jungle we did sight a few monkeys, lots of birds, even a crocodile, but the highlight of our trip to the lodge was the sighting of a rhinoceros! WOW!

We slowly approached the rhino—closer than you might expect. Rhinos are nearsighted but *he* seemed to be staring intently at us. He hardly moved but made sounds like a cat in heat—a surprising sound from such an enormous, fierce animal! As we sat quietly feasting our eyes on our rhino (the first of several we were to see), we were a little mesmerized, whispering to each other:

"Can you believe we're sitting on an elephant in the jungle of Nepal within 35 yards of a wild rhino?"

"Do you think he'll charge us?"

"It's like a dream becoming reality!"

We finally arrived at Tiger Tops and as Jumbo approached the lodge he didn't stop near the entrance but rather stopped parallel to the second level of the lodge. That was surprising! We more or less crawled off the platform into the helping hands of staff members. After sitting in our small box-platform on Jumbo's back for so long, it was not easy to stand up. In spite of that we succeeded without mishap.

The friendly staff took us directly to our rooms which were on the same floor that we had disembarked from Jumbo. They served tea and cookies and after seeing that we were comfortable told us that our meals would be served in the dining room on the first floor and announced the schedule. Our room, with thatched roof, was situated in a clump of magnificent trees. The building was so intertwined with the trees we felt we were in a tree house. So much fun! Even though we were surrounded with leafy trees, our rooms were clean, comfy, had electricity and hot water. We were told later that the facility was solar heated.

A bonus and unexpected surprise was that from our room we could look down to where the elephants were kept and tended, babies as well as adults. We spent as much time watching as we could. Especially fascinating were the interactions among the elephants and the care they took with their young ones. During our visit the staff held several sessions teaching us about these magnificent animals.

One most unusual and favorite adventure was going down to the river to "assist" the *mahouts* in bathing a few young pachyderms. It proved to be a hilarious, uproarious outing. The little ones were so excited to get to the water they ran toward it as fast as they could. And, my, oh my! After getting into the water they were so playful; frisky and frolicking. So much joy to watch—and to interact with! It was a very hands-on activity. We got nearly as wet at the little ones. We were like gleeful children getting to hold our first puppy; we simply couldn't get enough time with these amazing little elephants. Actually, the *mahouts* didn't really do much washing of the juveniles except at the end when we all threw buckets of water on them. And, yes, we were drenched when we returned to the lodge! It was one of those serendipitous moments which you always hope for but seldom materializes. But, WOW—when it does occur it's like a dream come true.

I had helped wash down a baby elephant several years before in Sri Lanka, but this experience was more satisfying, simply because we had watched the little ones from our room, had visited them in their living area and had even connected a bit with them. We had even given them names. We felt like we knew them.

During our time in the National Park we went on several nature walks, bird watches, but the elephant safaris were always the highlight of our days. Often when we left in the early morning and there was a thick fog in the air. It was eerie to see the elephants disappear into the mist, each going their own way. Near the lodge was a swamp and river we had to cross and one morning we were most fortunate that in the far distance we saw a tiger crossing the river.

On our second night at the lodge we had a not-so-pleasant outing. Near midnight we were taken about 30 minutes from the lodge to a blind. Looking out to an open area which was dimly lit we saw a goat had been tethered to a pole there. After a brief time, a tiger came out of the jungle and made a meal of that poor animal. It was horrifying to see; absolutely awful. We were told that this was done regularly for the guests in case they were not fortunate to see a tiger on their elephant safari. I still wish I had not seen this gruesome spectacle.

The day came too soon and our jungle-elephant adventure was over. It was time for Jumbo to take us back to the airport to catch our flight back to Kathmandu. On arrival, Jumbo kneeled; we climbed down, gave him several loving pats, and said our reluctant goodbyes to him and to our helpful *mahout*. It was time to leave. The plane came roaring in. A few passengers disembarked, we boarded and flew off into the blue knowing that we had just had an adventure of a lifetime!

This remains one of my favorite short trips of all time. My other favorite short trip was in Halong Bay in VietNam. But, that's another story for another time.

Above: Elephants in the mist at Tiger Top.

Below: We found our rhino—fantastic!

Chapter 18

NEW GUINEA: THE HULI WIGMAN
AND THE ASARO MUD PEOPLE

The year was 1988 and a friend and I flew into New Guinea for one of the most exotic and fascinating trips of my life. At that time Papua New Guinea (PNG) was one of the last unexplored areas on the planet and the second largest island on earth. The island is divided into two parts—eastern and western. The west is now part of Indonesia. The east, which was at one time part of Britain, Germany, Austria, and Australia, finally gained its independence from Australia in 1975. From the time of independence it became known as PNG.

Our adventures took us to the Huli Wigman tribe which was blissfully isolated until the 30s. The Huli are one of the largest ethnic groups in PNG and one of the world's most isolated societies. In some inaccessible regions of the island whites were not seen until the 90s! Natives had little knowledge of the outside world and initially it was thought that whites were "ghosts". The ghosts were evil spirits that had come to hunt them down, kill and eat them. It has even been said that in this off-the-beaten-track area the first wheel ever seen by the natives of PNG was the landing gear of a Cessna plane. Furthermore, today's transportation is still largely dependent on small aircraft, rather than surface transportation. There are reportedly over 700 languages spoken in the country and in some God-forsaken areas, living conditions remain a throwback to the Stone Age.

We landed in the capital city of Port Moresby where we spent less than six hours—having been warned before of the many dangers that abounded in the capital. After a brief meeting at a newly-formed travel agency, we flew up to Tari in the central highlands. Tari is tucked among the 13,000 peaks of the Mt. Hagen region—a region which is still often referred to as the "land of the unknown."

We landed in Tari on a dirt landing strip. There were no buildings. That landing tract, when not being used for planes, was (and still is) also used as a market for fruits, vegetables and other consumables. Additionally, it served as a community center for tribal gatherings.

We were driven by Land Rover to our lodge, the Ambua. It was one of the few accommodations appropriate for western tourists, and is still today one of the most famous lodges in the entire country. We were thrilled with our individual cottage. It was large and circular with a thatched roof. There were clean, wood floors, water and electricity. A glorious view of other cottages scattered in the lovely valley below made the scene very picturesque.

The Ambua Lodge was perched 7,000 feet above a peaceful valley of lush vegetation, flowering trees and colorful flowers. It was populated with a prolific variety of birds. When we arrived we were immediately aware of the sounds of all of those birds cooing, cawing and chirping. Each morning we were happily awakened with the melodious, sweet songs of these tiny, feathered creatures. It was a symphony of harmonious music, so soothing and tranquil. During our entire visit in PNG the beauty and sounds of the birds were absolutely amazing.

The next morning at breakfast, we were told by our guide we might have a rare opportunity to witness an amazing Huli "Sing-Sing ceremony" *if* we were willing. We were advised that to observe this ritual we would have to walk into the jungle for a mile or so.

There would be no other foreigners at the site. We were not to expect any danger; nevertheless, we should proceed with caution. The guide would be with us at all times.

We eagerly accepted this rare opportunity. After all, to view a tribal ritual that few foreigners had ever seen—how could we refuse? Indeed, viewing the Sing-Sing ceremony proved to be a stupefying, shocking experience. It was like a scene straight out of a Tarzan and Jane jungle movie.

There were approximately 1000 men, women, and a few adolescent boys. All had painted bodies of bright reds and yellows and were dressed only in loin cloths decorated with tail tufts from pigs. They were adorned with various other decorations. Adults were wearing spectacular head-dresses. The Huli are famous for these extraordinary headpieces. The region is known as the "Land of the Wig Men." Wigs are works of art and are made of real human hair and bird feathers. They require 18 months to construct. Hair is collected from all family members and packed tightly into a frame. The frame is then held together with woven strips and "watered down" to obtain the brownish color of birds. Elaborate decorations of bird feathers, bones, cowrie shells, and other fascinating ornaments are added to the wig. Upon completion the wig becomes each individual's own creation—a magnificent headpiece.

New Guinea natives were fascinated with birds. They were in awe and envy of the "lords of the air." Birds were (and still are) their role models. They develop dances, attire, sounds, and other rituals that emulate birds. The favorites to imitate are the five species of the Birds of Paradise. (Today, Birds of Paradise are a protected species throughout PNG.) Visually, it was a haunting sight to see a thousand aborigines with brightly painted bodies and regal headpieces stomping and oscillating to the rhythmic sounds of drums. It was incredible and unforgettable!

Natives stood in two parallel lines facing each other. Both lines were chanting and jumping up and down and sideways to drum beats, while also shaking large, dried pods as rhythmic instruments. They were emulating birds in movement and sound, especially the beautiful Bird of Paradise. Most natives appeared to be in some sort of a stupor—probably due to *khat* (an African or Arabian plant with amphetamine-like qualities) or cannabis. These drugs were and still are prevalent in the country.

Fortunately for us, at no time did we feel any discomfort or fright. We were ignored—as if they didn't see us. After filling our senses with this unforgettable experience of sight and sound, we departed from the scene. We were conscious of having encountered a spectacle that appeared to be straight out of a cannibal movie. We were elated that we had taken the small risk and had attended this astonishing Huli Sing-Sing ceremony.

Another exhilarating adventure was when a bush pilot flew the two of us deeper into the jungle. We landed on another dirt landing field in a seemingly uninhabited area with nothing to be seen except a small clump of trees and a river barely visible beyond the trees. When we disembarked from the plane and the pilot readied to leave, we expressed concern at being left on the landing strip—with no human life to be seen. He chuckled and told us, "Not to worry—someone will eventually come." With those few words he boarded the plane, waved at us—and flew off into the blue.

What to do? The sun was hot, so we walked over to the shade trees to get out of the heat and cool off. After a few minutes of discussing our unusual predicament and getting more anxious by the minute, a native appeared and with a big, wide smile said, in English, "Welcome." We were relieved! He picked up our two small backpacks and gestured for us to follow him.

After walking fifty yards or so, we came to the Karawari River (a tributary of the Sepik). There we found a small, flat-bottomed boat with a motor. The three of us settled into the boat for our trip up the river to our destination—the secluded Karawari Lodge. The guide navigated up the narrow, muddy river for 30-40 minutes, with few attempts at conversation. He didn't appear to speak English. Besides, it was too noisy. On each side of the narrow river was thick, dense foliage. The great, leafy branches of trees sometimes nearly covered the entire river. We were definitely in the jungle! We giggled a lot and said that we felt we were in the movie *African Queen*, traversing the Uganda River with one difference: our guide was hardly a Humphrey Bogart!

After leaving the boat we were led on a small path up a hill to our lodge which was perched on a ridge overlooking the river we had just traveled. We were greeted by a friendly and helpful staff dressed in colorful, native garb. The lodge was constructed of wood and bamboo with a thatched roof. Our room was within the lodge and was adequate. It was clean, with an indoor toilet, water and electricity. It was quite acceptable for a few nights.

The following day was spent on a motorized boat with a few other tourists going down the Karawari River to its source, the Sepik River. We stopped at villages along the river and disembarked. We were able to see natives going about their daily routines in their everyday attire. Women wore grass skirts. Most were bare-breasted and some had bones or other ornaments hanging around their necks. Men wore loincloths. A few were naked. Most mesmerizing, however, were the few that were wearing the famous *penis gourds*!

During dinner on our last night at that lodge we had another weird experience. As we were enjoying our meal, we were being entertained by music and dances performed by various native locals. Not particularly spellbinding except for their garments—or lack thereof. However, the last few minutes were riveting.

We were told that the staff had been scouring the jungle for a special native they wanted us to meet. By good fortune he had been located earlier in the day. With a statement indicating how incredibly lucky we were to have this opportunity, an abnormally fierce native slithered into the room. He was adored with beaks and feathers of the Bird of Paradise, and every other conceivable African ornament—including his penis gourd! He was introduced to us as "the world's only remaining headhunter." He certainly looked the part—hideous, horrifying!

We managed to appear mortified at this unexpected and bizarre event. But privately, we had our doubts that we had actually seen an authentic headhunter. Regardless, I had a picture taken standing next to him. (Until well into the 20th century some tribes were still practicing head-hunting—which involved bringing home the head of an enemy as a trophy.)

We had numerous extraordinary experiences in PNG—each one stranger than the last. However, one additional adventure merits recalling. It was a tour, unlike the Sing-Sing where we were the only outsiders. There were six of us on this tour. We were taken to see the ferocious Asaro Mud Men who live deep in the jungle. These Mud Men, or Ghost Men, were at one time revengeful warriors. They cover themselves from head to toe with grey mud and wear huge grotesque masks made of mud.

We were escorted to small benches to be seated. The dense jungle completely surrounded us. Shortly after we were seated and making light conversation with each other, out of the jungle emerged the most hair-raising, creepy, ghostly-looking creatures I'd ever seen. They silently crept toward us. Suddenly, they pulled out their bows and arrows and aimed at us. One of us screamed! (It wasn't me.) Hearts were thumping. This had not been expected! These evil, evil-looking creatures did not appear to be friendly, but after slinking to within ten yards of us they finally dropped their bows and arrows. They approached us and we quickly realized they were friendly. Whew!

On our return to the lodge we giggled, shared our thoughts and reflected on another uniquely entertaining day we had spent in PNG.

Papua New Guinea was like no other country that I'd ever seen, with the possible exception of a few regions in Africa. The culture is unique—exceptionally weird and bizarre. It remains drastically separated from the rest of the world as most of us know it. Largely unspoiled, it seems like something out of a prehistoric era.

Fundamentally, it is a "payback" culture. Attacks on men from different hamlets and clans are still common. (In earlier times Christian missionaries attempted, but had little influence in discouraging fighting and killing.) Usually, fighting was over ancestral lands, women, or pigs. Most likely, fighting was fueled by testosterone and the cultural traditions of the warriors.

Tribes lived in hamlets scattered around the jungle and living arrangements are unique, to say the least. Men and women lived in separate households, but usually within sight of each other across a sizeable garden or field. I never did figure out when they got together for "hanky-panky." After a baby was born, the infant remained with its mother and she nursed it for several years. The child was then taken to live with the father, permanently.

The women then had a "higher calling", another more important responsibility—which was to raise pigs. Why? Pigs are an enormous factor is this culture. As a payback culture, pigs are considered as wealth and used as paybacks, regardless of the purpose of the payback. The "Sing-Sing" ceremony we observed earlier was a payback event by a neighboring tribe. Our tribe had been guests of that neighboring tribe and had given several pigs as gifts to their hosts. It was time for the visiting tribe to "pay it back" by entertaining their hosts from the year before. (That particular event was a friendly pay-back.)

Twice during the two weeks we were in PNG we happened upon the haunting scene of woman in the jungle nursing a piglet. Mind-boggling! Needless to say, that vision is forever imprinted on my memory.

Markets in PNG were the most sparse I'd ever encountered offering hardly enough to sustain the population. There was little variety of fruits and vegetables and other edibles. The quality of the food was such that none of it would ever reach an American's table. Most adults that we saw in the villages and jungle appeared lethargic, malnourished or unhealthy. In all likelihood this was probably due to poor diets and living conditions. Sadly it's the only place that I ever visited that babies and young children were not cuddly or cute. One wasn't even tempted to pinch their cheeks or touch them. They were pathetic little creatures.

(I checked childhood mortality rates on several charts. Results varied. In the years 1985 to 1990, the mortality rate was 89% per

1,000 children under the age of 5 years old! The rate for the same demographic in 2012 was 63% per 1000. This statistic is much better, but still appalling. More recent rates could not be found.)

Papua New Guinea is on my bucket list of places where I'd like to return. I'm curious to see if the "modern world" has penetrated this macabre island and if the peculiar customs have remained the same.

Above: The Asaro Mud Men (Ghost Men), covered from head to toe with gray mud and huge grotesque masks.

Below: Huli Wigmen. Famous for elaborate head-dresses made from human hair and bird feathers.

Above: Warrior Ghostmen (Asaro) emerge from the jungle with bows and arrows.

Right: Huli Wigman with two "friends."

A native New Guinean taking a rest along the road.

A Huli mother nursing her baby.
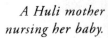

Above: Hulis at a "sing-sing." They are one of the largest ethnic groups in Papua New Guinea. Note the "glasses."

Below: A native village along the Karawari River.

PART III

MEMORABLE EXCURSIONS
AROUND SOUTH KOREA

Chapter 19

THE "VIRGIN" CAR

In August of 1968, I flew in a military plane from McCord Air Force Base to Inchon, a port city on the tip of the Korean peninsula. Other teachers and I were met by a Depart of Defense School administrator and taken directly to a large hanger on a nearby military base for processing. After several hours of intense heat (no air-conditioning), and filling out multiple pages of needed documents, we finally boarded the bus to be taken to Yongsan where the Eighth Army Base was located and where we were to teach. We were each assigned permanent quarters and within four hours of arrival I moved into a Bachelor Officer's Quarters (BOQ) room where I was to remain for two years—sharing the bathroom with another teacher.

Much to my delight, within an hour of moving into the BOQ, I was invited next door to meet other teachers, some of whom had been on the same flight with me from the states. Happily, those teachers became my good friends for the next 20-some years. We were known as the "adventurers" of the school. We traveled up and down the country hoping to learn more about the land and its people—and experienced more than our share of fun and extraordinary escapades.

Most American teachers never left the base except to go a block or two into Itaewon for shopping. Few Koreans off base spoke any

English and teachers were simply not comfortable when leaving the comfort and protection of the military base. On the other hand, our group had a great advantage through Ricardo, a very close friend. Ricardo had attended the Monterey language school to become an interpreter for the Korean War. It was our good fortune that he was so knowledgeable about the peninsula, a born adventurer and loved exploring the country and interacting with the Koreans. He became our resource for all things Korean—and was not only our friend, but our much respected and appreciated guide.

A few days after our arrival, school started. It was a new chapter in our lives and an exciting time. Meeting students, making new friends, decorating our BOQ rooms and finding our way around the military base—all made for a bit of chaos. Even so, we were thrilled to be living in Korea and thrived on it.

Nevertheless, within a few days of our arrival, our "bubble" burst. We received the unfortunate news that teachers would not be allowed to have cars—or any vehicles except motorcycles or scooters. Imagine there being *no cars*! We were told this topic had been in negotiations with base officials for several months before our arrival. Naturally, we had assumed that we could have cars. Consequently, the decision from base headquarters was a real shocker! We couldn't have cars—but we would be allowed to have motorcycles or scooters! Great. I could just imagine how happy my parents would be if they knew that I was riding a motorcycle around in Korea. Growing up in a small town in Oklahoma, a fine, upstanding young lady would never be caught riding a motorcycle—or even having her ears pierced, for that matter. So, I adapted.

For several months our motorcycle group travelled different areas of Korea, and in spite of the risks and difficulties of our trips we had a blast! I continued to ride behind Ricardo on his cycle, but will admit that I remained scared out of my mind from the very first to the last motorcycle ride! It should be noted that my first ride with three other bikers was on unpaved roads and at one time even involved putting our motorcycles on a raft to get across a river. There were few paved roads outside the capital city of Seoul. That first ride was a full day of discoveries, adventures and dirt-road hardships. It was 13 hours long! I still remember how my *kumtungi* (rear end) felt at the end of that day! In spite of the dangers, aches and pains, I persevered and I look back on that first trip and other ones with great fondness.

In mid-November, the long awaited announcement was made that teachers had been cleared to have private cars! WOW! I immediately took a taxi into the city to a newly opened car dealer, and on the spot ordered a brand new Datsun. That very day I gleefully started the countdown: 46 days, 45 days, 44, 43, and so on—until the car was to arrive. The big day came the first week in January. I could hardly wait to have "wheels of my own!"

I took a day's leave from school and prepared to make the trip out to Inchon where the car had been delivered. Hard to believe, but I was required to pick up a jerry can with gas and a couple cans of oil. Fortunately, I had requested and obtained written, detailed instructions on how to get to my destination. This was a necessity because of the language difficulties.

I took a base taxi to the Seoul bus station, lugged my gas and oil onto the bus and was ready and raring to go! I was going to pick up my car! No more motorcycle rides for me! Upon arrival in Incheon, I heaved my gas and oil cans into another taxi; gave the driver a paper with instructions on where I wanted to go, and off we went to my destination, the U.S. Military Customs Office. After filling out all the necessary paperwork, the customs clerk kindly picked up the gas and oil cans and told me to follow him to his military vehicle.

He said that we'd have to drive to a nearby beach where I would take possession of the car.

We drove through a guarded gateway to a sandy beach and stopped about 25 yards from the shore line. There were a few enormous "objects" scattered around the beach covered with what I'd call brown butcher paper. I wondered what those objects were. We got out of the vehicle and to my astonishment the customs agent started removing the paper from one of the objects. You guessed it! It was a Datsun—my car! That car had been unloaded from the boat directly onto the sandy beach! It had never been driven in Korea. What fun!

The agent put the gas and oil in the car; handed me the keys, said the car was mine—and wished me well in getting back to Seoul. Driving my own pristine car across that sandy beach, up to the paved road that would lead me back to big city was quite an adventure. I was "on top the world!" Such a unique experience!

However, getting back to Seoul was something of a nightmare. I had not gotten written instructions for the return trip thinking it wouldn't be necessary. Wrong! After all, anyone should be able to find her way back to the military base—even if the base was in the middle of a gigantic city of over nine million and I didn't speak the local language. It was not easy; not at all easy. But it was a "fun" nightmare, and finally, driving through the gates of the base that evening in my brand new Datsun car, I felt just like I just won the Daytona 500!

Chapter 20

KING MUNMU'S UNDERWATER TOMB

My first autumn season in South Korea (1968) we "Adventurers" took a trip over to the East Coast, near the magnificent Mount Sorak Range, a mountain range that extends up into North Korea. It was a rough 18-hour trip over all dirt and gravel roads, as were so many of our jaunts. We lived on a military compound in the center of Seoul, one of the largest cities in the world. We already had an understanding of "city life"; we relished our excursions into the countryside to learn more about the country folk. As usual, it was extremely taxing, with more than our share of flat tires and muffler problems.

We stayed at a *yeogwan* (Korean inn) in the village of Bonggil-ri, which means "middle of the sea". It was perched on a cliff overlooking the East Sea, also referred to as the Sea of Japan. Koreans have always been adamant that this sea should be referred to as the East Sea. To this day, they still object to name the Japanese gave it. They see is it as another Japanese "invasion" of their culture.

Our destination on this trip was to see the Underwater Tomb of King Munmu which is located in the water between the rocks of a beautiful islet some 100 yards from the shoreline. King Munmu lived in the 7th century and was able to unify three ancient kingdoms. He became the 30th ruler of the Silla Kingdom.

Before his death (681 A.D.) he gave specific instructions to be buried in the East Sea so that he could "become a dragon" and protect the Silla Kingdom from Japanese intruders. History tells us that Munmu did not achieve his objective. Japan has occupied the peninsula countless times since King Munmu's demise.

After settling into our *yeogwan*, we started out on our adventure, which was to find the area of the coast where that underwater tomb might be located. As we approached a beautiful and incredibly rocky coastline with a back-drop of glittering blue sea, we could see in the distance a small island. Immediately, we thought that this might be our destination, even though there was no one on the beach except a fisherman and a very old boat.

We approached the beach and cautiously walked toward the fisherman to inquire if the islet was where King Munmu's tomb was located. Fortunately, one member of our group spoke Hangul (Korean) and was able to convey to the man that we wanted to go out to visit the underwater tomb. The boatman told us that he'd have to make three trips because of the effect of the sizeable waves on his small boat. He could only take two of us at a time. Incidentally, that boat appeared to have survived from the Methuselah's time.

After haggling for a reasonable price, the first two of our small group were rowed through a rough sea out to the island. The fisherman then returned for the rest of us, making two more trips. Eventually we were all standing on the island at the same time.

Once we arrived we had a short, but difficult climb up to the highest point on the islet. The slippery rocks and the steep incline made for a dangerous and grueling climb. From the highest point, we were able to look downward toward the storied "Underwater Tomb of King Munmu."

This small island was divided by a cross-shaped waterway, forming a pool of water at the center. At the bottom in the center was a granite stone, said to be 11 by nine feet and over two feet thick. Legend is that the remains of King Munmu were cremated and were buried in an urn under this gigantic rock. It should be noted that historians still debate this issue.

Trying to balance ourselves at the top of the rock, we watched the stone intently. Every few minutes the water roared in completely covering the tomb. In due course it furiously rushed out until the surface of the tomb was visible again. We stood and sat on the rocks for nearly a half hour. It was a stunning day with brilliant sunshine and shimmering, iridescent blue water. Drinking in the beauty of our surroundings, we simply wanted to relish this uncommon, but powerful experience.

Our return boat trips in the swirling waters to the beach were uneventful. We had had quite an adventure. We were elated to know that we were most likely the first and only *waeguk-saram* (Korean for "foreigners") to have ever viewed the Underwater Tomb of King Munmu.

To this day, the underwater tomb is not one of the top tourist sights to visit in Korea. To my knowledge, only private tours can be arranged to visit the king's tomb. It continues to be considered too "off the beaten track" for tourists to make the effort to visit it.

Chapter 21

FARMER'S MARKET—
AND THE BOOBS!

The year was August 1968 and I was on my way to Korea. The prior year I had completed a one-year assignment with the Department of Defense Dependent Schools in Goose Bay, Labrador. I was now assigned to Seoul American High School at the 8th Army Base in Yongsan, Korea, where I was to be the music teacher at Seoul American High School.

I was happy to have left Labrador as it was not my idea of the most idyllic country. When covered with snow—which was most of the time—it was beautiful, but extremely remote. Happy Valley was the biggest town in the country, having a population of roughly 5,000, and was located a few miles from the military base where I worked. There were only two or three passable roads in the entire country. Recreational facilities were limited, which made for a long, long, cold, bitter winter. Teachers were assigned there for only one year because of the harshness of the climate. It was considered as a "hardship" assignment. It unquestionably lived up to its billing! Equally important was the fact that Labrador was often at 20 degrees below Fahrenheit, and on several occasions the temperature went to 40 below. When that occurred, all personnel living on base had to remain in the building wherever they were until the "all clear" siren sounded. When the temperature dipped to that extreme only emergency personnel were allowed outside. On occasion, this rule was broken resulting in dangerous and even life-threatening episodes.

I taught on the first floor of the school building and because of the mounds and mounds of accumulated snow, I could not see out the windows of my music room from late October to early May! In fact, school bus drivers were required to wait until children entered their houses, rather than just to wait until they left the bus and crossed the street.

Labrador was my first overseas assignment with the Department of Defense, but on that hot and humid day in August 1968 I was on my way to my second assignment—Korea. And, as was related in an earlier chapter, our flight landed in Inchon, Korea. Military personnel met us and transported us to a nearby military base for processing. After completing all needed paperwork, we boarded a bus and were transported to the military base at Yongsan, in the central part of Seoul, the capital city. School officials met the bus and assigned each of us to a Bachelor Officer's Quarters (BOQ). I was assigned a roommate; each of us had one room which served as our bedroom and we shared the bathroom. This one-room-sharing-bath arrangement continued for two years until each of us finally received two rooms of our own and a private bathroom. Several years later, when teachers received permission to live off base, I moved to a four-room apartment where I resided until retirement.

Fortunately, within two hours of my initial room assignment, I was invited down the hall to meet other teachers, several of whom had been on my flight. Happily, from that day on and for some 20 years, this small group of five-to-six became lifelong friends. We became known as what I'd call "The Adventurers". Happily, today we remain in close contact even though we're scattered all over the U.S.

The Adventurers were unusual in that we left the military base nearly every weekend to travel the peninsula to learn more about the people and its culture and to enjoy the improbable beauty of the country. It should be mentioned that even though the Korean

War had ended years before, most of the country was still in dire straits and not many *waeguk-saram* (foreigners) traveled far from the capital city. Many experiences could be told of our travels, but this one is of particular interest.

On this trip we traveled to the far southern part of the peninsula. We had the distinct impression that some of the locals had seldom seen *waeguk-saram* before. We assembled at a Bachelor Officer's Quarters (BOQ) on a Saturday morning and drove down country to the remote part of the peninsula. Traveling in those days was not easy, but we usually had three vehicles, so we were never without support should we need it. There were few paved roads outside Seoul, and on this particular trip we spent at least eight hours on the road. Finally, we arrived at a Korean *yoegwon* (inn) for the night. On our travels to the countryside, we often hauled our own gas and without question had more than our share of flat tires and muffler problems. These problems were always a constant.

Many of our trips to the country involved staying in Korean *yoegwons*. This excursion was not an exception. At that time there were few western accommodations except in major cities, and none in the countryside. *Yoegwans* were not known for their comfort, being lacking in basic necessities for a good night's rest. Rooms were more than grim. There was a chest in the room which held the bedding, mats to sleep on and lovely quilts for covers. A single light bulb hung from the ceiling. Outside our rooms were long troughs for washing and brushing teeth. There was no hot water. The outhouses were a distance away—thank the good Lord! The stench coming from these facilities was nearly unbearable. Frankly, I considered the toilets as "chambers of horror", cesspools to be avoided at all costs. You were confronted by a hole in the ground with a place on each side of the hole for your feet. That was it! Or there were rotting boards to sit on which were infested with roaches, spiders, ticks, worms, and every other despicable vermin in existence. It was nauseating—appalling—revolting! I usually tried to find a bush.

South Korea has a unique traditional way of heating buildings. It is a process of heating hidden water pipes that run under floors of structures. It is known as "*ondol* heating." Consequently, our bedding was placed on the linoleum *ondol* floors. That was all very well and we were used to it, but temperatures could not be regulated. In effect, you slept on one side until you felt that you had been totally fried. That forced you to turn over to fry on the other side. It certainly didn't make for a restful or comfortable night of sleeping.

At that time in Korea, there were only a few dishes that you could eat off base. As a result, on those trips we took our own food and drink. Two local dishes that we were able to consume "on the economy" (off base) were *olm rice* (hot rice with egg on top), and a few other smelly, fish dishes. A local brand, OB Beer, and a terrible imitation of Coca-Cola, were the only beverages that could safely be consumed on many of our jaunts off base. We carried our own water and "adult beverages".

On this particular trip we were on our way to the Horse Washing Pavilion but decided to make a side trip to the local Farmer's Market, like those which took place throughout the country. This was a special market in that it would not only have food, clothing, and basic farm necessities, but it would also have a large number of livestock in the market. We arrived and sauntered through the food and clothing part of the market, but were more focused in getting over to the livestock which was more unusual to us.

Korean farmer's markets are extremely basic. Stumbling around in this market—trying not to lose one's footing while plodding through piles of mud and animal poop—was not for the faint of heart. At this particular market there was a variety of goats, sheep, chickens, an ox or two, and other livestock. There were more cows than other animals and a bull in a nearby pen. Some of the cows were tethered, some were not. Thus, it was necessary to be alert at all times because of the danger of meandering cows and other farmyard animals. Picking our way about and trying not to lose our footing in all the dirt, cow patties and filth was not very enjoyable. Nevertheless, one of my favorites experience took place in this farmer's market.

As I was standing in the smelly mud—was never sure of its composition—I was distracted and was gazing at a commotion taking place across the way. I became aware of a tiny, tiny, old, grey-haired, and toothless woman. She was standing within a few feet of me, staring intently. She probably didn't weigh 70 pounds wringing wet, and was severely bent at the waist. This was likely due to spending a lifetime in the rice fields planting rice—one strand at a time. She continued standing quietly within a few feet, just looking at me. I was accustomed to this attention simply because I had blue eyes and blond hair, which was uncommon in the country. I was also stocky—"fluffy"— ample in stature. In Korea, if you had blue eyes, it was assumed that you couldn't see. Only dark eyes could see. Blond hair was also fascinating to Koreans in that it was seldom seen. Curious locals were sometimes insistent in wanting to touch yellow hair. This was a problem for some Americans and other *wae-guk-saram* who had young, toe-headed children. Attempts to touch those flaxen locks often frightened the young ones.

With the little old lady still looking at me, I continued watching the commotion across the market. Suddenly, I felt this hot little hand on my breast, pumping—pumping—pumping it for all it was worth. Talk about surprised—ohhh, my!

As I gained my composure, I observed that my little admirer was looking across to her *ajoomeonis* (her old lady friends) and was nodding her head vigorously. Without a doubt, she was indicating that my boob was real—and honest-to-God, *bona fide,* genuine breast! Wow! It was a known fact that Korean women were in awe at the magnificence of the American woman's anatomy. She was just checking it out to see if it was "real"—and it was!

Of all the many foreign markets I've visited in my travels, none brings a smile to my face as much as the experience at the "Boob Market" of Korea!

∾

I've had an abundance of stories of my many years as a music teacher and counselor in South Korea. Conceivably, at a later time I may write to share other explorations and learning experiences or discoveries of life in Korea—a country I grew to love. They were simply "too many" to include in this memoir. Even so, I elected to share the three stories above, which reflect some of the diversity of life in Korea.

Above: The spectacular coastline of Korea—near the island of Hongdo

Below: Ajoomeonis (old lady friends) in a Korean farmer's market.

The "Adventurers" of Seoul American High School.

PART IV

Miscellaneous Footprints

Chapter 22

IT WASN'T ALL FUN AND GAMES

I would be negligent, if I didn't mention a few of the not-so-fun situations that occurred during my travels. People say I must have been born with a "cast-iron-stomach" and I have been accused of having the bladder of a camel. I did have a rare few illnesses on my travels. Furthermore, it should be said that I was not at all selective about when I was ill. I couldn't have possibly chosen more inopportune times!

The most punishing episode was a 24-hour bus ride from Srinagar to New Delhi. The night before we were to leave on a flight for Delhi I had started feeling a little discomfort. This was totally unexpected. We had just finished our stay of a blissful week on the peaceful houseboats of Kashmir and had had no health difficulties, whatsoever.

Even so, when I arose the following morning I quickly realized that I was "in trouble". I immediately took an Imodium and didn't give my discomfort a second thought. At that time, Imodium was my favorite medicine for the "green apple quick-step." It had always worked in the past and just as important—quickly. In more recent years I sometimes take a daily Pepto Bismol when traveling.

However, shortly after we were awakened, with breakfast being served in our rooms, we had a rude awakening. We were told that Air India was having a nationwide strike. They advised us that the only way we could get back to Delhi (for an already confirmed flight out of India) was on a bus. We were assured that the bus would be comfortable even though it would be a long, long ride—24 hours. We were not overly concerned. After all, glitches in our travel plans had often been conquered before.

We packed up and set out for the bus station. Upon arrival and seeing our "comfortable bus", we went into a minor state of shock. The vehicle was one of those colorful, ancient, rusty, dirty, filthy, non-air-conditioned Indian buses that transport not only *homo sapiens*, but also every imaginable other small, four- and two-legged animal—and even fish. We boarded, squeezed into rusty seats—no padding. We immediately knew that this would be a bus ride of a lifetime.

Thankfully for me, the Imodium pill did its usual magic. I was "stopped up" for the entire bus ride. This escapade was horrendous and the bus ride, an epic 24-hours long. It was unforgettable, but one adventure which I'd like to forget.

The other incident was like a bad dream. Most travels in this memoir were not on organized tours. However, my friend and I had been on an organized tour of Morocco when this disagreeable nightmare commenced. Casablanca was our entry city to Morocco, after which we visited Rabat and Fez. It was in Fez that my friend became ill and was even confined to our hotel room for several days. She did not fully regain her health until near the end of our Morocco odyssey.

My nightmare started a day or so before we were to ride our camels across the desert to camp for the night. At the onset of my malady the problem was mild. I was not overly concerned. I definitely should have been! The day eventually arrived on our tour when we transferred from our vehicles, mounted our camels and rode off into the desert for several hours. My health problem had deteriorated and I was beginning to get a little concerned about camping on the desert. I was acutely aware that the toilet facilities would not be as convenient as in a hotel room. I somehow managed but eventually "Montezuma's Revenge" hit me a vengeance. A full blast! Unhappily, our tent was perhaps 20 yards from the closest tented toilet facility. Need I say more? Just be aware that it was truly a nightmare on a starry night in the desert!

(On the positive side of this trip, I did take my first hot air balloon ride over the desert!)

But enough about illness! Let's talk about the physical discomforts of a long flight!

When my father died I was living in Seoul, Korea, and I wanted to get home in time for the funeral. I couldn't get a quick reservation on a commercial flight, but was able to get on a Medevac flight. I'm not sure the type of aircraft, but it was one of those enormous cargo planes that serve as flying emergency ambulances.

The interior of the plane that I boarded was unlike those of commercial planes. There was no insulation in the plane, nor did it have the standard seats that are used in commercial flights. Most of the seats were bucket-like, rope seats which ran parallel to the length of the plane. Not comfortable. The plane was solely equipped for the wounded and ill. It was not for civilian passengers.

The plane was going to Tinker Air Force Base in Oklahoma, my destination. In addition to delivering injured and sick soldiers to various bases *en route*, there were mechanical difficulties and significant delays. It was a long and exhausting trip, but I made it in time for the funeral. It took 42 seemingly endless hours!

In my travels I've found that I can endure many difficulties and bumps in the road if my goal is attainable. For me, adaptability has always been one of the most critical factors in travelling. Another element has been managing unrealistic expectations that host countries will be "just like it is back home". I never felt the need to "Americanize" places that I visited. In other words, I've always tried hard to be a good American ambassador in all of my travels. I hope I succeeded.

Chapter 23

WHEN MY FOOTPRINTS
CROSSED THOSE OF VIPS

Wanderlust has not only led me around the world to unknown places; it also gave me opportunities to meet some high profile people which I would have never met had I not left my hometown.

Meeting Mother Teresa was the most awe-inspiring of those encounters. It was only by chance that I met her. I was attending a church service with a Catholic friend in the great Myeongdong Cathedral of Seoul, Korea. We were seated on the aisle near the altar. After the service ended, Mother Teresa walked down the aisle and stopped where we were seated. There were only a few Caucasians in the entire church—perhaps that's why she stopped. I was shocked to see she was a tiny, tiny woman in stature, but one with a kind face and large, piercing eyes. She spoke limited English, hence our conversation was brief, but it was such an extraordinary honor to even be near her!

Shaking hands with Presidents Richard Nixon, George H. Bush, and Bill Clinton was also a thrill. (You will have read the story of Nixon's visit to Ethiopia and meeting him in an early chapter of the book.) Several years later after I returned to Oklahoma I had the opportunity of shaking Clinton's hand—twice. Following that, in the 80s, George H. Bush visited Seoul American High School. After his speech he walked over to shake the hands of a few school personnel who were sitting on the front row. I was one of the lucky few.

I shared lunch and tea with Princess Julia Lee while living in Korea. That is also an enduring memory. Her Imperial Highness Princess Julia Lee, an American, was married to Prince Yi Gu of Korea. Their union was legally disputed and she was never fully accepted by the royal family. Nevertheless, she lived in the Imperial Household in Seoul until they divorced. After the divorce, while going through a difficult time due to those unhappy circumstances, she lived in my very modest apartment during the summer while I was in the states. She now resides in Hawaii. A few years ago the celebrated Ang Lee, director of the film "Crouching Tiger Hidden Dragon" and other outstanding films, was said to have initiated talks with Julia Lee about making a movie of her life. To my knowledge, that film has never materialized.

I cannot resist one more story of having had the opportunity to meet what I consider VIPs. Upon my return from Africa, I settled in Tulsa and started my music teaching career in the states. Shortly after my return a friend and voice major who I had known in college at OU encouraged me to join the chorus of the Tulsa Opera. Of course I refused, saying that I could sing but not at that high caliber. However, happily for me, she was persistent and soon, I gleefully became a member of the Tulsa Opera Chorus. By good fortune, in those days, you didn't have to audition. Consequently, I was easily admitted.

I sang with the chorus for several years and during that time an amazing number of world-class singers came to sing with the Tulsa Opera. As luck would have it I was actually able to meet and talk with a few of the various visiting VIPs. My favorite was Beverly Sills, an amazingly friendly woman. If a nickname was ever appropriately "assigned" to anyone, the name "Bubbles" perfectly described her. She was a joy to behold, both her personality as well as her phenomenal talent. Among others that I was fortunate to have performed with were: Roberta Peters, Dorothy Kirsten, Richard Tucker, Norman Treigle and possibly a dozen more.

PART V

THE POWER OF EDUCATION

Chapter 24

My Ethiopian Family

This chapter is not an account of my travels, yet it would not have taken place had I not traveled to and lived in Ethiopia. It is an on-going narrative of a scenario about how education is the thread that weaves through all my travels. It's the tale of how education presented opportunities to me and people I met. It's a chronicle of which I'm very proud to have been a small part. It is a story still in process.

My parents, who were employees of the United States Aid International Development, under contract with Oklahoma State University, lived in Addis Ababa, Ethiopia for nearly 12 years. Had they not stayed so many years in Ethiopia, this remarkable story would likely not have materialized. Nor would it have such a predictable and powerful ending. It is an account of the power of education— and of concern for others.

It was on one of those incredibly beautiful Ethiopian days in 1956 when David, a close friend, and I drove to the piazza in Addis to purchase the TIME magazine. There were no other book stores in the entire country. Every Saturday most *ferenji* (foreigners) in this capital city made a trip to the bookstore to purchase the TIME magazine. They might also buy other publications in English that had been approved by the Ethiopian government for distribution.

As we parked the Volkswagen an adorable Ethiopian boy about 11 or 12 approached our car. With a million-dollar smile that spread from ear to ear, he came running up to us and said, "No, Momma! No, Poppa! Me watch car." We were immediately charmed by this urchin and after haggling with him about the cost of watching the car we left him "to watch" and went about our business.

The following Saturday, as we neared the bookstore, the same ragamuffin boy ran out to the car with the same greeting: "No, Momma! No Poppa! Me watch car." Of course, we were already in love with this waif so we spent time with him asking questions attempting to find out more about him and his background. Our weekly trips to the bookstore and talking with our young friend continued on for weeks to come.

"How old are you?" we asked. He replied that he wasn't sure. "Where do you live?" we asked. His reply was that the last few years he spent most of his time in the Trinity Church compound, sleeping in the church or on the grounds of the church. "Where are your parents?" His reply was again disturbing. "No momma, no poppa. They finish." After more questions we were able to deduce that he didn't remember his father, and his mother had died several years ago.

We drove away that day determined to inquire around to see if there was any validity to his statements. Sadly, we found that our little friend, Tadessa, was telling the truth.

After some soul-searching, David, my friend who was a gentle and caring soul made a difficult and life-changing decision. That decision would have astonishing effects for years and generations to come. He made the decision to invite Tadessa to leave the streets and come live with him. The spectacle that followed was such a sight to see! Such exuberance—such jubilation I've seldom seen. Tadessa was literally jumping for joy in excitement and of course, he accepted without hesitation. Within days, Tadessa moved in with David, and at a later time his older brother, Gebeyehu, joined them. Several months later, another street urchin, Girma also moved in with them.

David not only took on the responsibility of providing food and shelter for the boys, he gave another equally important gift. He immediately enrolled them in school and was insistent that they attend classes daily. Previously, none of the boys had attended school on a regular basis.

Emperor Haile Selassie was a strong advocate for education. Under his regime he decreed that every child, boys *and girls*, had an undeniable right to an education. He issued a law of the land that education would be free for all up to the 9th grade. After moving in with David, all three boys attended school faithfully. They flourished. They were so bright and eager to learn that within a few years they began skipping grades.

The schooling and living arrangements for Tadessa, Gebeyehu, and Girma continued until David returned to the United States in 1959. Regrettably, David was never able to return to Ethiopia to continue formally mentoring the boys. Nonetheless, years later, all three boys, as adults, were able to visit him in the United States.

After David returned to the states, the three boys came to live with my parents and me. As expats (the nickname for expatriates: Americans living overseas) we followed the household traditions of the country by engaging household help. There were living quarters in the compound for domestic helpers. The boys lived in those quarters, attended school, helped around the house, and were treated as family members. There was always a great deal of interaction between my family and "the boys".

One of my favorite experiences with the two youngest boys was trying to determine their ages. The oldest boy, Gebeyehu, knew his age but the younger ones, Tadessa and Girma hadn't a clue when their birthdays were, or their ages. Because of their lack of this essential information, I made an appointment with a dentist and took the boys in for examinations. I had explained to the dentist one of my objectives when making this appointment.

After the dental examination, I asked the dentist, "How old do you think these kids are?" He replied that he couldn't be sure but he thought they were around the ages of 13 or 14.

After receiving this information, I turned to the boys and said, "OK, we need to give you an exact day on which you can celebrate your birthdays for the rest of your lives. What day would you like it to be?"

They looked at each other, grinned and gleefully replied, "We want our birthdays to be on July 23rd, Haile Selassie's birthday! Then we won't ever, ever have to go to school on our birthdays the rest of our lives!"

Happily, our mission to the dentist that day was successfully completed. As far as I know, from that day on both Tadessa and Girma continue to celebrate their birthdays on July 23.

It should also be mentioned that Tadessa had only one working eye. The other eye was glass. When asking him how he lost his eyesight, he had no recollection of how he lost it. Gebeyehu, his older brother did not know either.

My parents, through their association with Oklahoma State University (USAID), remained in Ethiopia for nearly 12 years— longer than any other Oklahoma State employees. That enabled them to see that after completion of high school each boy had the opportunity to continue his education. This was extremely rare in Ethiopia. At that time in Ethiopia, the illiteracy rate was 97%.

Below, I have given a brief account of each boy's educational achievements, as well as those of their children.

❧

Tadessa, the young street urchin who had watched the car on our weekly trips to the bookstore, graduated from high school and went on to Jimma Agricultural College to join his brother, Gebeyehu. After that he attended the Debre Zeit Veterinary College. He had a very successful career encompassing various jobs, but his predominate job was with International Livestock Research Institute where he was the Coordinator for the Debre Zeit Research Station. In conjunction with his job, he traveled extensively and spent a year of training in Ireland, but also trained and traveled to India, New Zealand, Holland, and Sweden. He married Yirgedu and they had three children: Biniam, Dagmawi and Tsegasellasie.

Below are the educational attainments of Tadessa's children:

BINIAM: Degree in Economics. He is the Marketing Manager for EST General Trading, PLC, and is married. He and his wife have a baby girl.

DAGMAWI: Graduated with Honors with a Degree in Graphic Design. Employed as Graphic Design Coordinator for African Phonebooks at Anypol International, he is not married but is looking.

TSEGASELLASIE: Earned his degree in Computer Science, and is currently enrolled at Georgia Tech for his Master of Science. He works for International Livestock Research Institute as an Information Technology (IT) Specialist. He and his wife have one boy.

Gebeyehu, the oldest boy, graduated from high school and subsequently attended and received a diploma from Jimma Agricultural College. (This is the college that Oklahoma State University first established in 1954.) In due course, he traveled to Yugoslavia for additional training. He held several professional jobs, but his major one was working for a government institute that supplied agricultural machinery. He also worked for a private organization that imported and sold machinery. He married Ayelach and they had three children: Anteneh, Meron and Zelalem whose educational attainments include:

ZELALEM: Has a degree in Computer Science. He is employed at Cybersoft, PLC as a Software Developer. Single, but looking.

MERON: Her degree is in Information Technology. She is the Senior Stewardess for Ethiopian Airlines and is married.

ANTENEH: With a degree in Marketing, he worked for the Bank of Montreal for several years. Now he is self-employed with a trucking business. He is married with two boys and a girl. He and his family live in Edmonton, Alberta, Canada.

Girma, the youngest of "the boys", graduated from high school and soon thereafter joined the Ethiopian Air Force. (Ethiopia and Eritrea were at war.) Sadly, during the time he served with the Air Force, he was imprisoned. Regrettably, after his release he never had the opportunity to attend college. Before his imprisonment however, he excelled as a mechanical electrician and was sent to Texas for a lengthy program to participate in special training. After being released from prison he married and he and his wife became owners of a small hotel-coffee business. They had five children: Misfin, Dawit, Demalash, Abebe, and Masresha.

Three of Girma's five children went on to college. His eldest son received a diploma in Engineering, the second son, a degree in Civil Engineering and the fourth son earned a degree in Computer Science. The third and fifth finished high school and attended college briefly but for various reasons were unable to finish and are successfully employed at this writing.

It has been an inconceivable blessing to observe and realize the power that education has made in the lives of Gebeyehu, Tadessa and Girma. David's and my family's decision to give homes and mentoring to the three young boys has rewarded us many times over. Those decisions positively influenced the boys *and* they were able to do the same for their children. Apparently, that new tradition will continue for generations to come!

Even so, there is a profound sadness that concerns another Ethiopian child that I was closely involved with. That child was little Aster.

One morning while we were having breakfast, we heard the crying of a small child who was sitting alone in the garden. After bringing the child into the house we sent for Lemma, our houseboy, to help us determine how this child came to be in our yard. We were shocked when he told us that the child had been left there by a woman who claimed that the child was his. The woman was a prostitute that

Lemma admitted he had visited "only once", but he vehemently denied that the child was his.

Unfortunately, from Lemma's perspective, the crying child had a particularly high forehead, as did Lemma. She was the "spittin' image" of her father. Nevertheless, he was emphatic saying he would not take responsibility for this child. It was not his! Yet, to us, it was clearly obvious to us that the little girl was undoubtedly Lemmas.

 My parents discussed the situation, and said to Lemma that he would indeed take responsibility for this child or he would no longer work for us. It was not a difficult decision for Lemma to make; he actually had little choice. Hence, little Aster came to live with Lemma and his wife, who was our house girl. They all lived in the servant's quarters, but the stepmother was not happy about the situation. She never fully accepted little Aster.

Aster spent most of her time with my parents and me. "The boys" were older and were in school so it was not possible to spend as much time with them as I did with little Aster. When I was not working we were inseparable. It must have been quite a sight for the Ethiopians to see us together. I was very white, "fluffy" (plump), and had very blond hair. She was as black as the ace of spades and tiny, tiny, tiny. She was five years old but weighed only 22 pounds. We spent many, many enjoyable hours together. She called me "Little Momma" and referred to my mother as "Big Momma".

The time came when I knew I would be returning to Oklahoma to get an additional degree in music education. I considered taking Aster with me. But, after much thought, I made the painful decision not to take her. It was a terribly sad time when I had to say goodbye to her, but I think the decision was the correct one. I never saw her again.

When I left, Aster continued living with my parents. She spent much of her time with them and they saw that she continued her education and helped with her homework. They truly loved her. Aster graduated from high school the same month that my parents returned to the states to live. Regrettably, from that time on, Aster's life went into decline.

After my parents left Addis, Lemma, his wife and Aster moved to the U.S. Embassy compound where Lemma worked as a houseboy. Sadly, after a year or so of working and living at the Embassy, he died. His wife, who did not work at the Embassy, was unable to continue living in the compound and was requested to leave. She left, abandoning Aster; neither was ever seen again.

Happily, we do know that Aster graduated from high school so she had considerably more education than most Ethiopians at that time. I have hoped that after living with my parents she may have acquired additional skills and competencies to help her through life.

When I became aware of little Aster's plight I wrote requesting that "the boys" attempt to find out where she went after being abandoned. They tried, but were unable to determine exactly what happened to her. It was thought that she had married and left Addis to live in a village south of the city. The rumor has never been verified and for her, my heart remains so very, very sad.

After I left Ethiopia in the 60s and my parents had passed away, I continued communicating with "the boys" via snail mail and an occasional phone conversation. A few years before I retired I made the decision to return to Ethiopia to visit "the boys" and meet their wives and children. I was living in Korea at the time and Ethiopia was only a few flights away. That trip was one of the most emotional and satisfying trips of my lifetime!

To see these young men and their beautiful families and to know their "stations in life" and the impact that David's decision to "take them off the streets" was astonishing! During my visit I had the unexpected opportunity of meeting a few teachers who taught Gebeyehu's, Tadessa's and Girma's children. We discussed their potential futures. The visit to the school was immensely gratifying.

Throughout the course of my visit, "the boys" treated me like an angel descended from heaven. They often told me they fully realized the dramatic, life-changing opportunities that education had made in their lives—*and* in the lives of their children. It was a tremendous validation of the power of education.

I retired to Seattle, Washington, in 1999. As David's and my finances permitted, we jointly brought Gebeyehu and his wife to Seattle and Tucson, Arizona (David's home) for a two-week visit with each of us. In due course, after a year or so of recuperating our expenses, we brought Tadessa and his wife for their two-week visit. We later attempted to bring Girma and his wife.

Unfortunately, Girma was unable to obtain a visa because of the political strife in Ethiopia. Consequently, his visit has never materialized. His wife is now deceased. Even so, it should be noted that in earlier years, during the time he was training in Texas he did have the opportunity to visit David in Tucson for several weeks. That visit coincided with my Spring Break and I was able to fly in from Korea to see him at that time.

Today, I am in contact with the young families of Gebeyehu, Tadessa and Girma on email and Facebook. Sadly, Tadessa and his wife have both passed on but Biniam, their oldest son, has been of great help to me in "filling in blanks" and doing some research for this narrative.

I have not been surprised to discover that Gebeyehu and Girma who are now in their 70s are not communicating on social media.

However, it is my good fortune that their children are. They have "friended" me, so I receive great joy in viewing pictures of their weddings, new babies, children's growth, and their daily lives on Facebook. And, I still get a thrill when I am sometimes referred to as "Granny" on social media or in the cards and letters I receive by postal mail.

The "boys": Girma, Gebeyehu, and Tadessa.

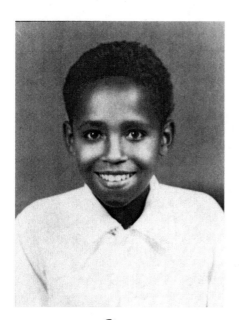

Girma

Gebeyahu

Tadessa

The three "boys" with children of Gebeyahu and Tadessa--and "Granny."
(Taken on my return trip to Ethiopia in 1996)

Above: Tadessa with wife and sons: Biniam, Dagmawi and Tsega Sellasie.
(Tadessa and wife are now deceased.)

Below: World Cup fans: The children of Tadessa and Gebeyahu.
(Picture taken during my return trip to Ethiopia in 1996.)

Above: The entire clan at Girma's house in Debre Zeit, near Addis Ababa.

Below: Adorable little Aster—who was rejected by both parents.

Chapter 24

ASSEFA + EDUCATION = SUCCESS

I would be remiss if I didn't mention Assefa Sahle Medhin, who has been not only a close friend, but a continuing source of information about "all things Ethiopian". For more than 25 years, Assefa was a very successful contractor in Washington D.C. He is now retired and lives part-time in Ethiopia and part-time in D.C. I have been in constant contact with him through the years via phone and email and he has visited me in Seattle. To this day he continues to email me newspaper and magazine articles concerning the current economic and social problems of Ethiopia. He is another example of a young life that was changed by the power of education.

Assefa was the last son born to his father who died of typhoid fever when Assefa was only two years old. His mother remarried after about a year and, in due course, Assefa became an older brother to six younger boys. He was never fully accepted by his step-father and eventually was sent to live with his grandmother in Addis Ababa. Even though he slept there, he was not attending school or eating well. By the age of nine, Assefa was completely on his own, except for that place to sleep. He worked at a variety of jobs which enabled him to purchase his own food, clothing and other necessities.

It was quite by chance that a neighbor observed his plight and enrolled him at a nearby school. Fortunately, he excelled in school and it was here that my friend David discovered him in a high school art class. He instantly recognized that Assefa was a bright young student with exceptional artistic talent. From that point in time, he continually and emphatically encouraged Assefa to pursue his remarkable talent.

After David returned to the states, my family continued with that mentoring and encouragement. We gave exhibitions of his artwork for the expat community and his work was purchased frequently. I have several of his pieces displayed in my home in Seattle. I knew Assefa and always encouraged him in his school and art work but was not as involved as my parents were in his life until years later, when I retired.

Emperor Haile Selassie had initiated an education program that recognized the brightest students in the entire country. After being identified, these exceptional students were given the opportunity to study overseas at accredited colleges and universities for five years— at the government's expense. Upon completion of their studies, students were expected to return to Ethiopia and work for two years in their chosen discipline for the advancement of the country.

Assefa was one of those selected for study abroad. He was given a choice of Germany or Paris. He selected Paris and attended the Conservatoire Nationale Des Arts et Metiers-Paris for two years. After his studies in Paris he came to the USA where he obtained an MSc in Architectural Engineering at Pennsylvania State University. After leaving Penn State, Assefa returned to Ethiopia where he became the General Manager of Building Materials Corporation. An enterprising man, he was also a private building contractor.

Assefa remained in Ethiopia until the political situation became increasingly desperate for the educated, due to the occupation of the Mengistu Communist regime. He soon realized that he needed to get his family out of the country before he and his wife were killed. (In Ethiopian history, educated people who were not in agreement with the political discourse of the time were often rounded up and murdered—either hung or shot.)

Assefa had written letters to me from Djibouti on several occasions while *en route* to Russia for supplies. He related that he was unhappy dealing with the Russians and the continuing decline in the quality of life and the political climate of his country. He became more anxious day by day about his and his family's survival. The next letter received from Assefa, who was again *en route* to Russia, communicated that he and his wife had decided it was too dangerous to remain in Ethiopia and they would soon try to escape from the country before they were killed.

A subsequent letter received from Assefa, who was again *en route* to Russia, related that he and his wife had decided it was too dangerous to remain in Ethiopia. Consequently, they decided to try and escape before they were killed. That was the last letter I received for quite some time.

A few years later I received a letter from him saying that he was in Uganda, employed as the Chief Executive Officer of the United Nations projects. His wife and children had reached Kenya where she was also employed as an official of the U.N. Several years later, he migrated to the U.S and subsequently became a highly regarded and successful contractor in real estate development.

A book should be written about Assefa. It is a story of "rags to riches", but suffice it to say that his story—like those of Gebeyehu, Tadessa and Girma—is but another which displays the enormous Power of Education and the transformation it made in their lives—and mine.

Assefa Sahle Medhin.
His life story is a tremendous validation of the power of education.
(Assefa now resides part-time in Addis Ababa and Washington D.C.)

POSTSCRIPT

I retired several years ago to the dynamic and beautiful city of Seattle, which I love. Happily, I remain in excellent health which allows for involvement with a wide range of volunteer, church and community activities. But, I do keep a "Bucket List" close at hand with the hope of having the opportunity to take "just one more trip."

High on that inventory is Easter Island, Antarctica, North Korea, Rwanda, Iran, Tel Aviv, and Papua New Guinea (West). It's a never ending list. Nevertheless, it's my hope that there's at least one more big adventure around the globe where my footsteps will lead me.

There are so many more travel stories that I'd like to share: Tashkent, Samarkand, Bhutan, the Balkans, Cambodia, Vietnam, Peru, the Amazon, and Dubai, Brunei. The list goes on and on, as do my memories.

It's been a delight sharing my travel adventures with you. I hope you've enjoyed them as much as I've had in recalling and writing about them. I'm fully aware that had I not received an education and left the comfortable confines of my cherished hometown, I would not have had the opportunity of seeing this astonishing world and learning about it's incredible inhabitants. I remain eternally thankful for those opportunities—it's been an amazing journey!

ACKNOWLEDGEMENTS

My memoir might not have materialized had it not been for the encouragement and exceptional skills of Sharee Wells, my editor. She is not only my editor, but I also regard her, her siblings and mother as "one of my own"— as family. She was indispensable in every aspect of my writing. Her expertise, knowledge and patience enabled me to complete a venture that I had only dreamed of attempting. I will forever be beholden to her.

Susun Wilkinson, her talented and accomplished sister, was the proofreader. Her analytical mind and discerning eye made sure that the manuscript was polished and professional. Though less time-consuming, her involvement was critical to the completion of the project and much appreciated.

I marvel at the twists and turns in life and the involvement of Sharee and Susun is one of those quirky happenings that was totally unexpected. I did not have the opportunity to see the girls often after their formative years, but a year or so ago our close association was reestablished, much to my joy. I only need to add that these sisters and their younger brother, Sam Stokes, were the youngsters who crawled into my bed, hid their heads and squealed as they listened to the stories of my adventures in Africa. What an amazingly wondrous twist in my life!

Additionally, I want to thank Gloria Campbell who taught the writing class, "Telling your Story", which compelled me to start my memoir. Her class was the first English class I'd taken since my freshman year in college. The class was important to the development of the book.

A big thank you to my designer and printer, Mr. Vladimir Verano. His expertise and skill have been invaluable in the production of this book.

A special *merci* to my friend Judy Michaels, who was a great listener throughout the trials and frustrations of this writing.

I particularly want to thank my childhood friend and soul sister, Sally Weiesnbach, for planting that seed of writing my memoir so many, many years ago. The book would not have happened if not for that seed.

Finally, though this list is not all-inclusive, I also acknowledge a number of friends, who shared my travels in this particular memoir and in other adventures. Such a limitless treasure of memories and knowledge I have because of these friendships and travels! In alphabetical order, they are: Al, Alice, Angela, Ann, Anna, Arline, Audrey, Beth, Bill, Bob, Bruce, Bunny, Charlotte, David, Diana, Ellie, Emi, Gayle, Hattie, Il Ling, Jackie, Janet, Joanne, John, Judy, June, Karen, Kathy A., Kathy W., Kay, Ken, Leslie, Lora, Lorraine, Louise, Lynn, Marcia, Mary, Marianne, Nancy, Pat, Pete, Ray, Richard, Ron, Roxanne, Roz, Ruth, Sara, Sarah, Sue, and Tom.

CPSIA information can be obtained
at www.ICGtesting.com
Printed in the USA
FFOW02n1450060618
47062989-49432FF